CHINESE IVORY SCULPTURE

CHINESE IVORY SCULPTURE

BY WARREN E. COX

AUTHOR OF

The Book of Pottery and Porcelain

BONANZA BOOKS

NEW YORK

THIS BOOK IS DEDICATED TO

Mrs. Frank Lewis Hough

who with her late husband collected many of the pieces
illustrated, and included in my exhibition of 1945 through
her kindness;

AND TO

Elizabeth AND *Ethelyn*

who kept things going while
I had the fun of doing it

TABLE OF CONTENTS

ILLUSTRATIONS IN THE TEXT

LIST OF PLATES

INTRODUCTION

THE sophisticated savants of our day have largely neglected the art of carved ivory in China. Bronzes they are interested in. Ancient carvings of jade and even of bone are considered quite respectable for a learned man to collect and to write about. But ivory is not understood or appreciated. This may be because many people think of Japanese carved ivories when the material is mentioned and associate with it the rather over ornate and detailed characteristics with which the Japanese treated it, and it is true that particularly in South China the Chinese also devoted their energies largely to multiplication of detail rather than greatness of conception and sureness of expression. However, when we go to North China and follow the art from its origin we find that strong and moving works of real art were created.

The material itself has always been rare and costly and has always been classed in the Chinese mind with jade and gold among the precious substances put to very particular uses. Perhaps this very rarity has somewhat contributed to the sparsity of collectors for, although we have a number of collections which comprise thousands of porcelains and potteries, we have practically no great collection of ivories in any way comparable. The collection of Mrs. Frank Lewis Hough is, therefore, outstanding. The Lucien Lion collection of Paris is largely of Ming and other uncolored pieces and the H. J. Heinz collection in Pittsburgh comprises several hundred pieces not all Chinese, and aside from these there are nothing more than a few scattered pieces in museums and private hands here and there. Mr. Ralph Dudley and I have worked for some years on bringing his things together and all told he has less than a dozen pieces. The great firm of C. T. Loo & Co. kindly lent me for my exhibition all they had,— some very beautiful pieces but far from many. (See the illustrations in this book.) Ralph M. Chait, another of our greatest American dealers in Chinese art had less than ten pieces, which he also kindly let me have for publication and for the exhibition. One might find one piece here and another there and that would be the sum total. The collector of ivory as it was carved in China is, therefore, not likely to build his collection very swiftly. The amount of money he is ready to spend will have very little bearing on the problem for there just are not many good ivories to be had.

Of course, the commercial ivory carvers of China have done their best to provide faked antique pieces nicely stained in an attempt to copy the beautiful natural color which ivory takes over a period of a few hundred years, but only a few comparisons are necessary to fix in the mind the differences between the natural restraint of ancient masters and the short-cuts of the commercial carver. It is hoped that the illustrations in this book will also aid in showing how the masters worked.

In my book on "Pottery and Porcelain," I spoke of the "tactile appeal" which a fine glaze has; that appeal which causes a Chinese collector to take a piece in his hands and run his fingers over it. The tactile appeal of an old ivory is even greater than of an old glazed pottery. This is because, first of all, the surface is a carved one and not simply a melted one. The carver can work exactly the soft change of planes and subtility of curves which he wishes.

He can also give just the degree of polish that he desires, while the potter has a more difficult medium and one which, in a large percentage of pieces, exhibits totally accidental effects. But the tactile appeal of a piece of old ivory gains in another way: the touches of many hands over a long period of years impart a warm, human quality to a piece of old wood or a piece of old ivory that is hard to describe, but that certainly adds to its charm, and no amount of staining and rubbing can produce the same effect.

In "Pottery and Porcelain" I also spoke of the appeal of a sort of challenging fragility which some porcelains possess. It is as though their very delicacy had protected them from rough handling down through the ages. If porcelains are possessed of this delicacy, carved ivories are to a far greater degree; and it is amazing, when one stops to think of it, that such pieces as Mrs. Hough has found have passed through many hands which instinctively were so appreciative of the appeal of fragility and respectful of the artistry and labor put into them that no slightest break has occurred.

Color is another of the basic appeals of fine ceramics and in color we find a wonderful appeal in the carved ivories of China. The application of color was not a recent thing; the wonderful, ancient hairpins which Mr. C. T. Loo let us have and which are illustrated on plate 4 are stained green, perhaps to emulate jade, and in almost every period from the Shang Dynasty (1783-1123 B.C.) when they were made, to the present we find that the Chinese stained their ivory carvings. They did not do this to copy other materials, nor did they try to make their ivories look older than they were by applying brown to them, as the commercial carvers do today; they simply saw the beautiful creamy material, found that it would take various stains which sank into it so that the grain was, if anything, improved and made more prominent, rather than covered up, and proceeded to add to their charm by the careful

application of color. The rare figure of the T'ang Dynasty (618-906 A.D.) in the Winthrop collection at the Fogg Museum of Art, Harvard College, has original staining on it, and others of each period are to be found. Only during Ming times (1368-1644 A.D.) was there a tendency to leave the material without color, but in the later periods the art was again resumed, and not every Ming example is free of stained or lacquered details. The purists may claim that the coloring of an ivory carving is like the gilding of the lily, yet these same purists accept the fact that most of the sculpture of ancient Greece was colored, and certainly no one can deny that the colored glazes add to the beauty of Chinese porcelains. In both cases the colors were opaque and actually hid the material from which the work of art was sculptured. In carved ivories the colors sink into the material just as stains do into wood and often bring out its hidden beauties. Again, the glazes of porcelains were often difficult to manipulate and their colors could not be very much shaded or toned. This difficulty is not met with when one colors ivory and some of the softest and most beautiful effects can be obtained.

We do not know what the Chinese used. I make a guess at some possible formulas in my last chapter, but this is a field of research which would be most interesting and rewarding. I sincerely hope that someone will make it his business to find out just what colors were used and how they were applied.

Such, then, are these beautiful works of art and little is known about them. The dating of an ivory is difficult and not much research has been done in this field. Dr. Berthold Laufer wrote a small book, now out of print, in which he gives more than anyone else. Mr. Arthur de Carle Sowerby wrote several articles for the China Journal, published in 1936, which speak of the sources of ivory as a material, the styles of carving and the Frank Lewis Hough collection in particular. Dr. George Frederick Kunz wrote a book "Ivory and the Elephant," published in 1916 and which is now also out of print. To these three sources I am largely indebted.

For the iconography which is most interesting in this field of art, and particularly for aid in obtaining data on the Eighteen Lohan, I am indebted to Mrs. Antoinette K. Gordon who recently published the excellent work "The Iconography of Tibetan Lamaism."

Much remains to be done and this book, it is hoped, may serve rather to stimulate further research and interest, than as any conclusive authority on the subject.

CHINESE IVORY SCULPTURE

I. Sources of Ivory

GENERALLY speaking, ivory is the hard, bone-like substance of the tusks or teeth of certain mammals such as the elephants or *Proboscidea*, as they are scientifically called, the hippopotamus (*Hippopotamus amphibius*), the walrus (*Odobaenus rosmarus* and *Odobaenus rosmarus obesus*), the narwhal (*Monodon monoceros*) and to a lesser degree the boar and the wart-hog or any of the genus of wild hogs *Macrocephalus*. It is a kind of dentine or tooth-substance of great toughness, elasticity and evenness, usually but not always covered in its natural state with a harder cement as hard as the hardest porcelain or glass, and made up of tubules which radiate from the central pulp cavity outward to the periphery of the tooth. To quote the Century Dictionary, "The most valuable ivory is that obtained from elephant's tusks, in which the tubules make many strong bends at regular intervals, resulting in a pattern peculiar to the proboscidean mammals." (see Pl. 1) And again, ". . . besides the fine angular radiating lines, it shows on cross-section a series of contour-lines concentric with the axis of the tooth, arranged about a central grayish spot which represents the calcified pulp. The appearance of these contour-lines is due to the regular arrangement of minute spaces called *interglobular*. Ivory in comparison with ordinary dentine is specially rich in organic matter, containing 40 per cent. or more." Of this wax-like substance we shall have more to say later. Of the elasticity, it can be said that slender whips have been made of thinly pared ivory. Of the hardness of the outer coating, Sir Richard Owen states that the layer of enamel on the outer side of hippopotamus tusks is so hard, "as to strike fire with steel."

Many kinds of ivory exist and many names both ancient and modern have attached to them. As we go along we will investigate some of these in detail but suffice it at this point to speak of a few, some of which will not interest us further:—"*Green ivory*" or "*Live ivory*" is that which has been freshly cut from recently killed animals, usually African elephants, and which is warm in color, translucent and dries out much lighter. "*Fossil ivory*" is, as one would suppose, quite dark brown due to the action of the ice and frozen soil in which it has been encased for some 50,000 years or so. Ivory is extremely sensitive to sudden extremes of temperature and about half of the "*Mammoth ivory*" sent to London from Siberia is rotten. "*Asiatic ivory*" from the Asiatic elephants, is on the other hand of a denser white and is more open of grain and softer than "*African ivory*," when it is green, if you get what I mean. Many names refer to ports of shipment. Thus "*Malta ivory*" is a term used although no ivory bearing animal occurs on the island. There are two main types of African ivory, the "*Hard ivory*" from the western half of the continent and the "*Soft ivory*" from the eastern half. The first is "glassy" and translucent while the second is duller and contains more moisture and stands changes in temperature better. The trade term for *Hippopotamus ivory* is, "*Seahorse teeth*" although the animal is never found in the sea and is called a "*River horse*" by some. "*Fish teeth*" are Walrus tusks, although the name was also used to refer to Narwhal tusks by the ancients at times. "*Narwhal horns*" are also spoken of though the tusk is a true tooth as we shall see, and bears no resemblance to a horn-like growth. Of types which we might mention in passing but which will be of no future interest to us in this treatise there is *"Artificial ivory"*, a compound of caoutchouc, "India rubber" or a thick, elastic gum obtained from the sap of various tropical plants, sulphur, and some white material such as gypsum, pipe-clay, or oxide of zinc, *"Brain ivory"*, the substance of the otolites or ear-stones of some fishes, and *"Vegetable ivory"* from the South American nut.

FOSSIL IVORY AND THE MAMMOTH

Of the elephants and their earlier ancestors we shall treat in the second chapter in some detail. Meanwhile since the *Mammoth* is the chief source of fossil ivory let us examine this fellow. He is one of the largest of the *Proboscidea*, a family name derived from the long nose or proboscis which is an outstanding characteristic, and his name is synonomous with gigantic or immense. The largest specimen we actually have according to Arthur de Carle Sowerby, to whom we are indebted for much of our information, stands some 13 feet 6 inches high at the shoulder and was an Imperial mammoth (*Elephas imperator*) which inhabited the Western and South-western United States and Mexico, but animals may have existed which were well over 14 feet high. Certainly it must have been a tremendous animal which carried a tusk such as that found near Mexico City which measures 16 feet 6 inches long. The longest tusk found in Texas measures 13 feet 9 inches and in Siberia 13 feet 7¾ inches. These latter belonged to a Columbian mammoth (*Elephas columbi*) and the best known and most numerous northern Asiatic ones called "*Elephas primigenius*" or the first elephants, although actually the mammoth is a late comer of the Pleistocene times. He is contemporary with the straight tusked *Elephas*

namadicus, another fellow which measured between 13 and 14 feet in height and inhabited the whole area between India and Japan. He was on the earth roaming along the northern ice-cap when our present day elephants of Europe and Asia came into existence. He was always a cold climate animal. Of course the usual tusks found measure only about 10 feet 6 inches in length and they are all rather slender in comparison with the tusks of African elephants.

These tusks are interesting and unique in their spiral curve for the roots diverge from one another, the middle part turns upward and outward and the tips on old individuals turn inward toward each other actually tending to cross. Obviously they were one of the useless exaggerations of nature, nowhere nearly so efficient as the tusks of present day elephants, and quite possibly hastened the extinction of the mammoth.

We have a very clear idea as to what these animals looked like because they were also contemporaneous with the earliest period of human development, the Old Stone Age or Paleolithic culture, when men had learned only to chip out rough stone implements and not to polish them, and these early ancestors of ours drew amazingly life-like pictures of them which have later been proven accurate by the finds of actual animals encased in frozen mud and ice. Here I quote Mr. Sowerby in one of the strangest stories we know, "One of the most famous of these is the Beresovka mammoth, which was discovered in 1901 in a remarkable state of preservation partially buried in a cliff of the Beresovka River, a tributary of the Kolyma River, some 200 miles north-east of Stredne-Kolymsk and 800 miles from the Bering Strait. It had evidently fallen into a cleft anywhere up to 50,000 years ago, breaking one of its fore legs and the bones of its pelvis, and had become frozen in and later buried, finally to be exposed once more by the action of heavy rains and discovered by a native Siberian hunter. An expedition was sent from St. Petersburg to salvage what was possible of its remains, and in due course the whole animal was restored and mounted in the Imperial Academy of Sciences in St. Petersburg. Between the time when the Lamut hunter found it and the scientific expedition recovered it considerable portions of the perfectly preserved flesh were devoured by bears and wolves." The excitement of the scientists can well be imagined but think of the awed wonder of the hunter who might not have ever heard of any such monster! It is not difficult to see why ancient men found an encounter with such an unbelievable animal an episode worth careful recording. I show herewith some of the drawings which occur on the

Fig. 1. SKETCHES OF THE MAMMOTH—TOP *sketch shows an engraved picture found on a piece of mammoth tusk in the Cave of LaMadeleine, France, having been done by Palaeolithic Man.* CENTER *drawings were done on the walls of caves in the Dordogne, France, also by Palaeolithic Man.* BOTTOM *a drawing by Mr. Arthur de Carle Sowerby from the restoration of a mammoth.*

walls of caves in Europe, while others were scratched onto stones, bones and bits of the animal's own ivory.

The average animal of the *Elephas primigenius* is said by Sowerby to stand about 9 to 10 feet in height. It has a very high forehead and crown and high, humped shoulder, a comparatively small ear, brush-like tail and is heavily built. The skin is covered with a yellowish brown wooly hair through which projects long, black or reddish brown, thick hairs forming patches on the cheeks, flanks and abdomen and reaching almost to the ground, as described by David Meredith Searles Watson. Thus it was not only well protected against attack but against the bitter cold of its habitat. It is the only proboscidea which preferred the colder climates; its relatives preferring the warmer climes of India and other southern countries. It is said to have had ample food in the thick vegetation of the areas in which it lived and it is difficult to establish what might have caused its extinction.

The name mammoth Sowerby says is a corruption of the name given it by the natives of Siberia, who call it *mamant* or *maman.*

It must have occurred in large numbers for the supply of ivory from tusks found is amazing. Sowerby wrote in 1936 in the China Journal, September issue, that, "Only a few years ago a large shipment of 140 tusks was received in London," and the Encyclopaedia Britannica 14th edition states, "The store seems to be as inexhaustible as a coalfield," and goes on to say that up to 1900 about 10 to 20 tons were received annually in London. These Siberian deposits have been worked for nearly two hundred years and they extend throughout Siberia although the richest deposits seem to be about the Lena River and others which flow toward the Arctic Ocean.

Other types of fossil ivory occur such as that of the ancient relatives of the present-day narwhal but it is rarely found and of no particular importance. The living narwhal, however, is of some interest.

NARWHAL IVORY

The *Narwhal* belongs to the order *Cetacea* or whales. It is an *Odontoceti* or toothed whale, although most of its teeth disappear soon after it is born, and is of the *Delphinidae* or dolphin family. Its own name is *Monodon monceros.* Our common name for it Dr. Berthold Laufer has said is from Old Norse *nahvalr* or Swedish-Danish *narhval, hvalr* or *hval* meaning whale.

Fig. 2. NARWAHL—*The Narwhal or Monodon monceros in which the left upper canine tooth develops into a long, twisted tusk.*

It is an interesting mammal resembling the white whale in shape, with head rounded in front and no dorsal fin, but small for a *cetacian* reaching only from about 12 to 16 feet in length. The body is mottled gray on top and white beneath. It is never seen south of Bering Strait or the parallel of 65° N. latitude except in the rarest of circumstances depending perhaps upon storm conditions. The strangest thing about it is that it loses all of its teeth except that in the male the left upper canine tooth and sometimes also the right upper canine tooth, but never the right without the left, develops into a long spirally twisted tusk which turns always from left to right and which passes through the upper lip projecting forward to a length almost equal to that of the animal itself.

This tusk is of fine quality ivory, being dense, hard and pure white not inclined to change to yellow or brown as it ages, but it is of limited value for besides being small in diameter the central cavity runs to about two thirds of the total length. Sowerby says the longest known tusk belongs to Major H. A. Steward and measures 9 feet 4½ inches in length. The thickest one he says is only about 3¼ inches in

diameter. The average tusk is about 8 feet long. Thus they can be employed only for making small objects. However, there is a regular trade into China from Kamschatka. Some of this is "dead ivory" washed ashore and some is fossil ivory, but most of it results from the hunting of it by the natives with harpoons from their small kayaks.

How this strange development took place in the evolution of the animal is not known and, in fact, the actual use to which the tusk is put is only a matter of conjecture. If it is a weapon, it has never, so far as is known, been used to attack the boats of fishermen as is the sword of the swordfish. Some have suggested that it might have developed to aid in cracking ice so that the creature could come up to breathe, but other polar whales get along without any such instrument. Again it has been suggested that it might be used in killing fish or possibly in combat with other males in the process of mating, but few if any actual observations have been recorded, and the former belief can hardly hold against our sure knowledge that the chief food is cuttlefish and crustaceans.

The old whalers have stated that it occurs in small schools and is very playful probably not unlike the other dolphins. These schools are usually led by one old bull who seems to be able to communicate his orders perfectly to the other members and to give complicated orders that are carried out. Of course much of this may be imagined by the observers but it must not be forgotten that some whales have brains not only larger and heavier than human beings but also showing more convolutions, and it has been said that, if these animals had happened to climb trees and then learned to run erect rather than return to the sea as they did, it might quite possibly have been they rather than men who could claim to rule the earth. Their hands developed into flippers to aid them in swimming while ours developed a thumb which made it possible for us to handle tools.

WALRUS IVORY

Walrus ivory is coarser than either narwhal ivory or hippopotamus ivory but has been sufficiently valued for centuries to lead almost to the extinction of this mammal. Sowerby gives record of the longest tusk known from Rowland Ward's "Records of Big Game" as 37¼ inches for the Greenland form and 35⅝ inches for the Pacific form, "the latter being that of a tusk taken from an animal off the coast of Kamschatka." Dr. Berthold Laufer says that they "sometimes attain a length of 20 inches or more and a weight of from 4 to 6 pounds." He further states that, "The tusks do not form a solid mass throughout, but are hollow about two-thirds of their length, so that large objects and billiard-balls cannot be carved from them." He adds that the outer layer is "hard as glass", dark in color and fluted. Thus the outer coating must be about as hard as that of hippopotamus tusks. The solid tips are yellowish and in cross-section have speckled designs while lateral cuts show fine yellow lines or, "flamed spots." On long

Fig. 3. THE WALRUS—*The walrus or Odobaenus rosmarus after a sketch by Arthur de Carl Sowerby.*

exposure this ivory turns yellow-brown. The pattern of its structure is quite different from that of any other ivory. The animal itself is the largest of its order excepting only the elephant-seal of the South Pacific and Antarctic Oceans. It attains a length of some 12 feet, the record being 12 feet 8 inches for a bull, and a weight of about 3000 pounds.

The walrus belongs to the order of mammals known as *Pinnipedia* which contains the seals. There are three families in this order: 1. the *Otariidae* or eared seals, 2. the *Phocidae* or seals, and 3. *Trichecidae* or walrus. This genus *Trichecus* contains two species or races, the typical form *Odobaenus rosmarus* which extends roughly from Hudson Bay eastward to North Europe and Siberia to about the Lena River or longitude 130°, and the *Odobaenus rosmar obesus* which occurs along the coast of Eastern Siberia in the Northern Pacific as far south as Kamschatka and east to the coast of Alaska.

It has been known by the natives for centuries, having been hunted by the Eskimos of North America, and the natives of the Aleutian and Kurile Islands, of the Okhotsk Sea and of Northeastern Siberia. Laufer says that long before the discovery of the Arctic shores of North America and before the two animals were described in our natural history, an extensive traffic in the ivory of their tusks was carried on all over not only Asia but also Europe. Of course the native hunters were chiefly after the blubber but that the ivory also interested them is proven by the primitive carvings which they did of this material, and much of it has been traded through Vladivostok to China and Japan.

Dr. Berthold Laufer (Ivory in China, Anthropology Leaflet 21, Field Museum of Natural History, Chicago) has made a special study of early sources of information concerning the walrus and some of his remarks may be interesting here. He speaks of a London publication of 1693 in which it was mentioned as an *Equus marinus* or "sea-horse" (This is not to be confused, of course, with the trade name for Hippopotamus tusks called "Sea horse teeth") and of others which termed it a sea-ox, sea-cow and sea-elephant, and as a morse or mors (a word of unknown origin). William Baffin in 1615 speaks of, "peeces of the bone or horn of the sea unicorne" (probably narwhal) "and divers peeces of sea mors teeth." — Still earlier and probably the first use of this word occurs in the Chronology of England by Caxton, 1482, in which it is said, "This yere were take four grete fisshes between Erethe and London, that one was callyd mors marine." But the first acquaintance of England with the animal itself was in A.D. 890 when the Norseman Ohthere made a report to King Alfred the Great of England saying, "The principall purpose of his travelle this way, was to encrease the knowledge and discoverie of these coasts and countreyes, for the more commoditie of fishing of horse-whales, which have in their teeth bones of great price and excellence: whereof he brought some at his return unto the king. Their skinnes are also very good to make cables for shippes, and so used." (See Anglo-Saxon translation of Paulus Orosius' History of the World.)

Dr. Laufer points out that our Anglo-Saxon word used in this text is *horshwael* from the Old Norse *hrosshvalr* meaning "a kind of whale" and *rosmhvalr* or "walrus" as it sounds in reverse. He gives a number of other interesting old references and goes on to say that in Russia walrus tusks were known as "fish-teeth" for the animal was classified as a fish in olden days. He speaks of an account of 1549 (S. von Herberstein's "Rerum Moscovitcarum Commentarii") which tells of the Turks making handles of daggers from "fish-teeth," and again of a book by Richard Chancelour ("The Book of the Great and Mighty Emperor of Russia" 1553) which says, "To the north parte of that countrey are the places where they have their furres—There also are a fishes teeth, which fish is called a *morsse*."

Dr. Laufer also quotes the Arab, al-Beruni (A.D. 973-1048) in a treatise on precious stones who called walrus ivory *khutu* and said that they traded it from the Bulgars of the Volga who brought it from the northern sea, and that they made knife-hilts of it. He says, "The Jesuit Avril observes that the Persians and Turks bought up walrus teeth at a high value and preferred a scimitar or dagger haft of this precious ivory to a handle of massive gold or silver." There was also an idea that ivory was an antidote to poison and that also added to its value and Laufer continues, "From a statement in the history of Akbar the Great, known as the Akbarnama, it appears that about 1569 a Raja in Malabar, who probably was the Raja of Cochin, sent Akbar a knife which had the property of reducing or removing swellings, and that Akbar told his secretary that it had been successfully applied in more than 200 cases. Probably this knife was made wholly or in part, of walrus ivory, which could easily have been brought to Cochin by sea."

Nothing directly is known about the use of walrus ivory in India but Laufer points out that a yellow sort looking as if crystallized into patches is called "fishtooth" in every dialect (*mahlika-dant*) which suggests, "at once a common and, most probably, foreign origin for the material."

There are many other accounts in the excellent treatise by Laufer but they all add up to the facts that little was known about the animal, its tusk was often confused with the "horn of a unicorn," and that was also confused with the tusk of a narwhal, it was very precious and sometimes more highly valued than ivory—or in some instances gold, it was also at times confused with the tusks of the hippopotamus and it was a more or less constant element of trade. He speaks of a "horn" found by an English sea-captain in 1611 for which the sum of two thousand pounds sterling was refused by the Company of the Greenland Merchants of England. It is true that they did not receive this amount but the thing was cut up and some twelve hundred pounds was realized.

HIPPOPOTAMUS IVORY

Hippopotamus ivory is dense and white though not so much so as narwhal ivory. Still it is as good as the best of elephant ivory and far better than that of the walrus. Owen says of Hippopotamus canine teeth that they consist of, "an extremely dense, compact

Fig. 4. THE HIPPOPOTAMUS—*The hippopotamus or as his scientific name is, Hippopotamus amphibius, after a sketch by Arthur de Carle Sowerby.*

kind of dentine partly defended on the outside by a thin layer of enamel as hard as porcelain; so hard as to strike fire with steel." Little porcelain is as hard as flint and this may be a slight exaggeration but the substance is very hard no doubt rating between feldspar and quartz or number 6 to 7 on the Moh's scale. The tusk is considerably more curved than either elephant or walrus tusks, is triangular in cross-section showing a triangular form in its grain when cut across and is much larger than the walrus tusk, the record length being 64½ inches for a lower tusk as recorded by Rowland Ward or nearly twice as long as the record of 37¼ inches for a walrus tusk. It, of course, lacks the structural pattern which looks like "engine turning' on the back of a watch which is found in the ivory of the proboscidea, that is elephant and mammoth ivory. While the walrus tusks which develop into great size are those of the upper jaw, it is those of the lower jaw of the hippopotamus which become largest though the upper ones are also well developed.

The animal itself, a very large, amphibious mammal, is allied to the hogs and, is known by the scientific name of *Hippopotamus amphibius.* According to Sowerby it reaches a length of 14 feet, height of 4 feet 10 inches at the shoulder (although the E. B. gives 3′10″) and a weight of about 3000 pounds, and spends most of its time in deep water coming ashore to lie about on sand banks and to feed on marsh verdure or water plants largely at night.

The body is heavy and broad with short legs and broad feet each having four toes. The short neck supports a long head with huge and particularly broad muzzle and cheeks. The arrangement of the protruding eyes, the nostrils and the small upright but flexible ears make it possible for the animal to breathe, see and hear above water while the rest of the body is completely submerged. The mouth is almost as wide as the body and with a wide gape which makes it possible to gather in huge masses of waterside plants and of the juicy stems, leaves and roots of water plants at a single bite. The skin is exceedingly thick, tough and is hairless, reaching a thickness of 2 inches in places. As Sowerby says it has been specially used in the making of cruel whips, called sjamboks, much in favour with the Boers of South Africa. It has also been used extensively by the natives for the making of shields of great strength and durability.

Formerly hippopotami were plentiful in all of the rivers of Africa. Now they have been entirely driven from the lower waters of the Nile and can be said to exist in large numbers only in the Zambesi, the Chobi, in Lake Ngami and throughout Central Africa.

In Pleistocene times, that is at the culmination of "The Ice Age" when the last continental ice sheets were receding and man had begun to make crudely chipped stone tools, had a primitive spoken language and had learned to use fire, a hippopotamus inseparable from *Hippopotamus amphibius* inhabited the greater part of Europe, while the dwarf species were found in the Mediterranean islands, Northern Africa, India and Burma. The antecedents do not particularly interest us, but a note should be made concerning these pigmy hippos called scientifically *Choeropsis liberiensis*. They are now found in Liberia and nearby parts of West Africa and are only about 6 feet long and about 2 feet 6 inches high at the shoulder reaching a weight of about 400 pounds. Although they are in many ways like the larger species their ivory is little used by the natives and has no commercial value, the tusks reaching no very great size.

There are a number of ancient references to the animal but the best known one and perhaps the earliest is that in the Book of Job in which it is called Behemoth.

With our modern weapons it is not very difficult to hunt the hippopotamus for its nature is mild and inoffensive but a wounded animal or one protecting its young can become aroused and is then very ferocious having an immense strength and surprising agility. Old bulls have also been known to become "rogues" as elephants do and attack without provocation. These are usually found alone but as a rule the animals are in herds of from 20 to 50 seemingly under the leadership of one large male. Their characteristics make them naturally dominant in their environment.

Aside from the *elephant* (and its ancient relative the *mammoth*) the *narwhal*, the *walrus* and the *hippopotamus* there are no animals which have produced ivory of any real value, although the tusks of *boars*, of the *wart-hog* and some similar animals have been carved by various natives.

II. Elephants and their Ancestors

NATURE is always making experiments and it seems that nothing is too exotic or extreme to be given a trial. Strangely enough some of the most exaggerated forms turn out to be successful; the long legs and exceedingly long neck of the giraffe help it to survive because it can reach the tender foliage of low trees in a country where grass is sometimes sparse and the strange hump of

Fig. 5. FOUR ANCESTORS OF ELEPHANTS—LEFT TO RIGHT: *Moeritherium, Egypt, Eocene Paleomastodon, Egypt, Miocene Tetrabalodon, Nebraska, Pliocene Elephas columbi, Nebraska, Pleistocene. An idea of the relative heights can be had when it is known that the last stood some 13 to 14 feet high.*

the camel and its great, padded feet make it possible for it to live in desert country where other animals would succumb, but of all the strange exaggerations of nature which have turned out to be entirely successful perhaps those of the elephant are the strangest. Who could possibly imagine, if he was not already acquainted with the facts, that an animal could reach such a position of dominant success in this world by the means of developing a long nose and upper lip, and two long and curved front teeth? Yet that is just what happened for the earliest members of the elephant family had no such noses and teeth.

So far as we now know the first ancestors of the elephant the genus *Moeritherium* were found in Upper Eocene deposits in the Fayum of Egypt. This is the period which geologists place just after that of the dinosaurs; the period, that is, of the very dawn of

life which resembles present day life and it occurred millions of years ago. This *Moeritherium* didn't resemble an elephant any more than the little *Eohippus* resembled the modern horse. *Moeritherium* looked more like a living tapir, was not very large, had a snout that was only slightly flexible while its canine teeth were also small.

Later in the *Lower Oligocene* of Egypt we find a more developed ancestor in the *Palaeomastodon* or early Mastodon, and here there are several species the largest of which is almost as big as our present elephant. His second incisor is enlarged but directed forward and downward, while, although the nose has elongated, the under jaw seemed to have jutted further forward than the upper and must have been used for grubbing around on the ground, and the neck is long and flexible.

Still later, in *Lower* and *Middle Miocene*, the time of the greatest development of larger mammals, in Europe, North Africa and as far east as Baluchistan we find *Tetrabelodon*, which has the beginning of a real trunk and looks very much like an elephant except that his neck is longer and his tusks are still pointed downward, while his lower jaw is still longer than that of the *Palaeomastodon*. As David M. S. Watson writes in the Encyclopaedia Britannica, "It seems evident that the enormously elongated jaws of the Tetrabelodon developed as an adaptation to allow the animal to reach the ground, when as a whole it was increasing in height whilst its neck was becoming shorter." Finally he tells us that in *Tetrabelodon longirostris* the ancestors of our modern elephants gave up trying to reach the ground and came to depend on their trunks for eating and drinking, the

25

lower jaw was rapidly reduced in size so that the trunk could hang down vertically, the lower tusks become short and rounded and the upper ones grow still larger and turn outward.

The later *Mastodons* become more and more like elephants generally speaking although there were many variations and side branches to the development, such as are found in the *Stegodons* and the *Dinotherium* an animal with exceptionally long legs and trunk. Some of these extinct variations are amazing. Thus the *Stegodon ganesa* which ranged from the Siwalik Hills through China and into Japan in the same period, had enormous tusks some 12 feet or so in length. The *Trilophodon productus* of *Upper Miocene* over 1,000,000 years ago in Texas had four tusks, two in the lower and two in the upper jaw, which almost anyone would agree must have been impractical and cumbersome. And Dr. Roy Chapman Andrews in 1928 on the Asiatic Expedition of the American Museum of Natural History, in Mongolia discovered in *Pliocene* strata, which would indicate that it was about 750,000 years old, the remains of the *Platybledon grangeri* or shovel-toothed mastodon which had, to quote Dr. Arthur de Carle Sowerby, "two lower incisor teeth greatly elongated and flattened out at the ends, so that together they formed a regular shovel as large and very much the same shape as that used by a coal-heaver." All of these experiments of nature failed in themselves yet out of them were developed our present day elephants which should truly have the title, "King of Beasts," far more than should the lions.

Our present day elephants have the scientific name *Proboscidea* which in a broader sense can also be applied to some of the older forms. Only in the last 30 to 40 years have primitive *Proboscidea* been found capable of comparison with other mammalian forms. The general characteristics of our living elephants are as follows:—The head has developed a long proboscis or elongated nose which is flexible and can be moved in any direction, and which is terminated with one or two finger-like processes so well controlled that, as we all know, even so small an object as a peanut can be handled. This proboscis, called a trunk, can also be wrapped around large objects and can exert great strength due in part to the animal's great size. It is capable of very accurate movement and is used in feeding. Actually it is not only the nose but this organ plus the upper lip, and the skin along its lower surface is essentially a part of the palate. The openings of the nostrils are at the tip of the trunk while the mouth is comparatively small and short. Some elephants have a single pair of enlarged incisor teeth called tusks about which we have more to say in our section on ivory. Of course the head has to be large and set upon a short and very strong neck to support the trunk and tusks and particularly to take the great strains which are put upon them when the animal lifts heavy logs or uproots trees. The skull is short but deep and the front part is made up of spongy bone, like the human sinuses, filled with many air pockets. The molar teeth move forward replacing each other as the front ones wear out and it is said that in a lifetime about a yard of solid tooth is thus worn out.

About the sizes of elephants we shall have more to say later but even for their great size the ribs are very long and enclose a capacious thorax. The leg structure is also interesting for the humerus (the bone from elbow to shoulder) is very long and much longer than the forearm so that the elbow is relatively only a little higher than the wrist of a horse. Moreover these strange animals actually walk on the tips of their fingers and toes but the palms and soles are so enlarged and padded as to take some of the load.

There are two distinct species of existing elephants, the *Asiatic elephant* and the *African elephant*. The Asiatic elephant is also known as the (*Elephas maximus*) and the *Indian elephant* (*Ele-*

Fig. 6. ASIATIC ELEPHANT (LEFT) and *Fig. 7.* AFRICAN ELEPHANT (RIGHT)—*The Asiatic elephant is the Elephas maximus. Note small ears and short tusks. The African elephant is the Loxodonta Africana. Note the large ears and long, heavy tusks.*

phas indicus) although subspecies inhabit also Burma, the Malay peninsula, Cochin China, Ceylon and Sumatra. The African elephant (*Loxodonta africana*) is found in most of Africa south of the Sahara, and also has several subspecies. The classification of the members of the elephant family is chiefly based upon differences in their large molar teeth. To quote Sowerby, "In the present day elephants and the mammoth these teeth have a flat grinding surface and are formed of laminated folds, which are most compressed and numerous in the Indian elephant and least compressed and fewest in the African elephant. In the mastodons and stegodons the grinding surface is composed of cross ridges of conical cusps, which are comparatively large and few in the former and smaller and in many more rows in the latter." And again, "In all of these there are pairs of well developed tusks in the upper jaw only; but in some of the earlier more primitive proboscids there were long tusks in the lower as well as the upper jaws." But there are other marked differences between the two types of living elephants.

THE INDIAN ELEPHANT

The Indian elephant is smaller than the African species, a full grown bull is about 9 to 10 feet high while a female is about 8 feet high. The "Records of Big Game" by Rowland Ward accounts for a bull in Burma 10 feet 6 inches high and one in Calcutta 11 feet high. The Indian elephant is also proportion-

ately shorter and heavier with shorter head and a higher and more pronounced forehead and smaller ears. There are 5 nails on the forefoot and 4, or sometimes 5 on the hind one. There is also a pronounced depression across the back of the neck and the trunk is smooth, not having the transverse ridges which occur on that of the African species, and it has only one fingerlike process at its tip. The subspecies vary, that of Ceylon usually having no tusks and the Sumatran variety being taller and thinner with longer trunk in proportion.

Sowerby gives the record tusk length as 9 feet 10 inches, the length of one in the Royal Siamese Museum at Bankok. Two others are known which measure 8 feet 9 inches and 8 feet 6 inches and both weigh just about 160 pounds. The Encyclopaedia Britannica gives a length of "nearly 9 feet and a weight of 100 lb., whilst the African elephant tusks may be 10 feet in length, with a weight of 220 pounds." Thus the average tusk of an Indian elephant is considerably less heavy and thick in diameter than that of an African elephant. It is also to be noted that only the males have large tusks in Asia, the females having very small ones or none at all, while in Africa the females also have large tusks which they use in feeding.

There has been a misconception concerning the natures of the two sorts of elephants. Most people are under the impression that Indian elephants are gentle and tractable while African elephants are wild and cannot be tamed. Actually this difference does not occur as an inherent trait and African elephants have been tamed, as we know, and used in war by the Carthaginians and Romans. They have also been trained to work quite as well as have the Asiatic ones. Partly the difference in some individuals, and it must be made clear that elephants have as much individual character as have house-cats, may be due to the treatment they have received. Carl Akeley was a good friend of mine and I remember many years ago he

27

told me something that has always stuck in my head since, "Animals don't like to be shot at." Men sometimes forget this simple fact. The Indian elephant naturally likes dense foliage, particularly in hot weather, and he seeks the thickest forests keeping in the neighborhood of water. While the African species also like the forests, they have a greater propensity to wander out into open country where, alas, they can be more easily hunted. Also nature in developing and bestowing upon them larger and more beautiful tusks did not take into account that the descendants of the ape family would learn how to make little metal tubes into which explosives could be put which would accurately throw a small pellet of hard metal sufficiently far and sufficiently hard to kill this great king of beasts. Thus while thousands of Asiatic elephants have been hunted and killed, their chief value rested in their being captured alive, while the African elephants have been massacred without restraint for centuries.

Sowerby says, "Ivory and slaves were the two great articles of trade which tempted the Arab traders and raiders from the north into the depths of Central Africa, the Congo region and on south of the Equator to the more open country beyond. . . . Here the ivory trail becomes one of blood and misery, and we see strings of wretched negro prisoners carrying the gleaming white tusks they had gathered in their hunts being driven by their fierce Arab captors to the sea coasts to be sold into slavery in foreign lands, and leaving behind them smoking villages and the dead bodies of their tribesmen." He continues, "When white hunters first came, sometime early in the 19th century, they found elephants abundant in the open country of South Africa, where it was possible to hunt them on horseback, and, being armed with firearms, the slaughter they committed was terrible. So much so, indeed, that soon after the time when men like the famous Frederick Courtenay Selous came upon the scene, the elephants had retired into the more heavily forested regions further north, known as the "fly" country, where the presence of the deadly tsetse fly prevented the use of horses, and hunting had to be done on foot." He speaks also of W. D. M. Bell who from about 1900 to 1931 had killed 1,011 elephants, and concludes, "WE ARE NOT VERY FAR FROM THE END OF THE IVORY TRAIL."—"Extermination faces the African elephant just as relentlessly as it did the mastodons and the mammoths of by-gone ages, and, even if various Governments decide to protect what is left of the once vast herds of the former by setting aside great game reserves in which it will be forbidden to kill them, IVORY WILL BECOME INCREASINGLY RARE, since there will be no further sources of supply." . . . Thus in a roundabout way it has been the salvation of the Asiatic elephants that their tusks are small or that they have none, for men found they could get more out of them by keeping them alive. Such are the strange workings of fate!

The Indian elephant does not breed readily in captivity and thus most of the tamed ones have been caught. This is done by building a funnel-shaped palisade of large tree trunks with an opening at the small end into an enclosure. The herd is driven into the enclosure where certain selected ones are cut out by tame elephants and training begins. Some eventually learn to love their *mahouts* and seem to enjoy working. Luckily they have no other commercial value than their tusks.

THE AFRICAN ELEPHANT

Some of the characteristics of the African elephant have been touched upon in the foregoing as they compare with those of the Indian elephant. The African species, called also *Elephas (Loxodon) africanus*, or *(Loxodonta africana)* has been subdivided into eleven subspecies by Richard Lydekker but we need not go into these as the differences are in most

BASE OF STAND FOR CRYSTAL BALL—The base of the stand for a crystal ball shows clearly the "engine turned" sort of design formed by the small tubes. It was cut from a small tusk about midway showing the natural hollow as it tapers near to its point. This illustration is about twice natural size. *Ralph Dudley Col., Warren E. Cox Galleries.*

PLATE 1

instances slight. The dwarf elephant of the Congo (*Loxodonta fransseni*) which stands only about 5 to 6 feet high when full grown is the only outstandingly different one. The basis on which the subspecies are determined is chiefly the size and shape of the ears, though also by differences in the shape of the skull.

Generally speaking the African elephant is larger than the Asiatic elephant, standing some 10 to 11 feet high. The highest point is in the middle of the back and there is no depression across the back of the neck. The trunk has many transverse ridges on its top and forward surface and is equipped with two finger-like processes at the tip. The largest animal given in Rowland Ward's "Records of Big Game" was 11 feet 8½ inches in height. The heaviest known pair of tusks are in the British Museum and weigh 226½ and 236 pounds although they are only 10 feet in length. The longest pair are in the United States National Museum, Washington, and came from Kenya Colony, East Africa. They measure 11 feet 5½ inches and 11 feet but together weigh only 293 pounds. In contrast the record for the Congo dwarf elephant is 34¼ inches in length and 4 pounds, 12 ounces in weight.

AFRICAN ELEPHANT IVORY

We have spoken briefly of the African elephant ivory in our first chapter. Let us now examine it more carefully :— The substance is actually between bone and horn, being less fibrous than bone and less easily splintered. It is composed of small tubes filled with a gelatinous or waxy solution which aids in the polishing of it. We have said that these tubes bend and radiate outward from the center and it is they which give the typical marking which best resembles the engine-turning sometimes applied to the back of a watch. (See PL. 1) The Encyclopaedia Britannica says, "Elephant's tusks are the upper incisor teeth of the animal, which starting in earliest youth from

a semi-solid vascular pulp, grow during the whole of its existence, gathering phosphates and other earthy matters and becoming hardened as in the formation of teeth generally. The tusk is built up in layers, *the inside layer being the last produced.*" This is the more amazing when one tries to figure out how the outer layers expand without cracking as the tusk grows larger from the inside. It is then seen why the substance has to be elastic to allow for this expansion.

A large part, perhaps a third more or less, of the tusk lies imbedded in the bone sockets of the skull and a hollow of conical form tapers to a point from about a quarter to a full half of the length of the tusk. This continues as a thread almost to the point of the tusk and is referred to as the nerve. It is easy to see, therefore, that even these great African elephant tusks afford only a limited size and shape in a single piece carving and one begins to appreciate the difficulties even in finding the material to do such a figure as the one illustrated which is some 30 inches high (See Pl. 20) or of the tremendous vase (See Pl. 19) which measures 27¾ inches high and 6½ inches in diameter and is straight, which meant that the curve of the tusk had to be allowed for. Such pieces are outstanding in scale alone, aside from their wonderful artistic merit.

Commercially most of this African ivory was used for billiard-balls, cutlery handles, piano-keys and toilet articles. Luckily plastics have largely taken its place in some of these categories but piano-keys and billiard-balls will probably continue to be made of ivory so long as it is available. In fact the latter account for the chief market. Small tusks called in the London market "scrivelloes" are employed for making billiard-balls. These are of the best quality soft ivory and weigh only less than 7 pounds having to be necessarily of the proper diameter. It is seldom that more than 5 blocks can be got out of a tusk, 3 of first quality, 1 of second and 1 with the bark on. Of course the more round and straight the tusk the better. The balls are partly turned and then left to season for five years finally being turned dead true. They are bleached, as pure white is considered desirable, although this takes out the gelatine and makes them more likely to crack. The Britannica says that a number of large dealers carry a stock of 30,000 balls at times. . . . At least it can be said that no part of the ivory is wasted for small bits are used for inlays and even the dust is used to make a food called ivory jelly, and in the preparation of india ink and the oil color called ivory black.

III. Elephants and Ivory in Pre-Han China

ALTHOUGH no pictures of elephants or other works of art portray them at any such early period in China as do those of Palaeolithic times in Europe, stone implements have been found, according to Arthur de C. Sowerby (Chinese Ivory Carving, Ancient and Modern, The China Journal, August 1934), with fossil elephant remains of Pleistocene age in the Ning-hsia Fu district on the border of Southern Ordos, or actually southwest of the Desert of Ordos about latitude 38°, longitude 106°, on the Huang-ho or Yellow River. Thus earliest man may have known elephants and also may have used ivory in China.

The earliest period from which we have actual ivory carvings is the Shang-Yin (1783-1123 B.C.) and I reproduce here a small piece illustrated by Dr. J. G. Andersson in "Children of the Yellow Earth" published in 1932. It was found in An-yang in the north part of Honan province and this along

Fig. 8. Ivory carving of Shang-Yin Dynasty (1783-1123 B.C.) from An-yang.

with other pieces published by Dr. LiChi and others prove very definitely that there was by this time a long established tradition in ivory carving. That the elephant was living in this section at this time is

proven by a sliver from a young elephant's molar tooth found in the "Waste of Yin" near An-yang in a Shang Dynasty site, and is now in the Shanghai Museum (R.A.S.) according to Sowerby. Dr. Berthold Laufer (Ivory in China, 1925) further substantiates that the Chinese knew the elephant well for they have an old indigenous word for the animal. It is *dziang* or *ziang*, while in modern dialects it is *siang, ziang, tsong, siong* or *ch'iong* in various dialects of the North, of Shanghai, Canton, Hakka and Fukien, while in Burma it is *ch'ang and* in Siam, *chang.*

Laufer also points out that the written symbol was conceived in the era when writing was purely pictographic and shows the following seven forms the last of which dates about 100 A.D. and is very close to the modern form :—

Fig. 9. ARCHAIC SYMBOLS FOR ELEPHANT AND A MODERN CHESS-MAN WITH THE ELEPHANT CHARACTER— *Archaic forms of the written symbol for elephant, the last dating about 100 A.D. (Han Dynasty) and similar to modern chess-man character as used today.*

Sowerby gives more prepared by H. E. Gibson and he makes a further claim that the elephant must have been domesticated as is indicated by the pictograph for *(wei)* meaning "to do," which shows a hand in front of an elephant, although I must say that I do not think this is necessarily a sound argument. Anyone observing an elephant would see that he uses his

Fig. 10. *Pictographs of the Elephant of the Shang Dynasty (S), on Chou Bronzes (C. B.) and in the Shuo Wen (S. W.). The Pictograph for Wei, "to do," shows a hand in front of an Elephant, "indicates that this animal was domesticated by the people of Shang." Prepared by H. E. Gibson*

trunk as a hand and possibly that is all that was meant to be suggested i.e. simply that this animal does things with his trunk as we might with our hand. Mr. Sowerby is not prone to stretch his logic as some savants do in their enthusiasm to prove a point but I should want more evidence in this case to convince me that actual domestication was meant.

The illustration from The China Journal article "Ivory Producing Animals" as Sowerby shows it raises an interesting point for speculation. Dr. Laufer states in "Ivory in China": "While the ancient Chinese were acquainted with the elephant and used its ivory for various purposes, it must be stated, on the other hand, that they do not seem to have taken a deeper interest in the animal. It played no role whatever in their mythology and gave no rise to religious conceptions. It may even be questioned whether the elephant was hunted by the Chinese themselves." He goes on to say that none of the ancient descriptions of hunts speak of elephant hunts, except, "The passage in Mong-tse, that Chou Kung, who died in 1105 B.C., 'drove far away the tiger, leopard, rhinoceros, and elephant to the great joy of the people.'" He concludes, "It is more probable that the elephant was usually hunted by the aboriginal 'barbarous' tribes, who sold the ivory to the Chinese or with it paid their taxes to the imperial government, and that much was 'dead' ivory (of animals which died a natural death in the jungle) ."—"Above all," —and this observation bears out the point in question,—"the ancient Chinese never made any effort to tame or train the elephant."—He sustains this by stating, "It was only in 121 B.C. that the first elephant was sent to the court of the emperor Wu of the Han dynasty from Nan Yüe; that is, the country in the south east, at that time inhabited by tribes of Annamese origin. The commentator of the official Annals of the Han Dynasty, Ying Shao, feels obliged, with reference to this passage, to define what a tame elephant is, 'It is docile, can make obeisance and rise again, and quickly grasps man's intentions.' This, accordingly, was something entirely novel to the Chinese." Of course Dr. Laufer's argument is not absolutely conclusive either, for it is quite possible that domestication might have taken place at some distant, early time, and that we have not come across the records of it to date, but I incline to agree with Laufer until further evidence is forthcoming.

Fig. 11. PICTOGRAPH ON AN-YANG BONE—*A sentence shown by Sowerby which reads, "Last month the rain stopped. This month it rained again and we captured an elephant."*

33

Backing his side of the argument Sowerby shows a pictograph fragment found on a bone at An-yang which he translates as follows, "Last month the rain stopped. This month it rained again and we captured an elephant." But, of course, the animal might have been taken dead or alive, and capture does not prove domestication. Here the matter must rest at present.

Certain it is that from the Yangtze Valley south, and north through Honan to the middle valley of the Yellow River, wild elephants were in existence in Shang-Yin times (1783-1123 B.C.) and unmistakable drawings of them are incised in bronzes of the period. These, as can be seen by those illustrated, are naturalistic while those of the Chou Dynasty (1122-247 B.C.) are in hieratic, strongly conventionalized form, although the modeling of the animal for bronze ornamentation is usually easily recognizable even in the later period.

Fig. 12. TWO ELEPHANTS DEPICTED ON SHANG BRONZES—*The elephant to the left was depicted on a bronze vessel and that on the right on a bronze bell dating about 1500 B.C. Both are of the Shang Dynasty (1783-1123 B.C.).*

The most interesting one shown by Laufer and which I illustrate on this page, is on a bronze bell found in Shantung Province and inscribed with the name of an emperor who reigned between 1506-

Fig. 13. ELEPHANTS DEPICTED ON CHOU BRONZES— *The elephant to the left appears on a bronze beaker "ku" while the symbol to the right is on a bronze vessel, both of the Chou Dynasty (1122-274 B.C.).*

1491 B.C. The rim is decorated with a row of elephants a picture of one of which was first published by L. C. Hopkins in "Development of Chinese Writing" (1909) from which Laufer reprinted it. Two examples of the Chou Period are given below for comparison.

Fig. 14. ELEPHANT HEAD MOTIVES USED IN ORNAMENTATION OF CHOU BRONZES—*The elephant head to the left projects from the corner of a bronze while the placing of elephant heads back to back in the design to the right forms a t'ao t'ieh "monster mask" on the side of a bronze vessel. Both of Chou period (1122-247 B.C.).*

Whether the "elephant goblets" of the ancient Rituals (*Li ki* and *I li*) were adorned with ivory or made in the form of an elephant or carried a design of an elephant we do not know, but it is sure that many bronzes carry more or less conventionalized elephant-head decorations and at least one well known vessel of Chou period, and probably Early Chou at that according to the more recent methods of dating bronzes, is made in the form of an elephant.

FIG. 15. CHOU BRONZE RITUAL VESSEL IN THE FORM OF AN ELEPHANT — *The only Chou bronze vessel I know actually made in the form of an elephant. Note the t'ao t'ieh design on the side. (Louvre, Paris). See page 36.*

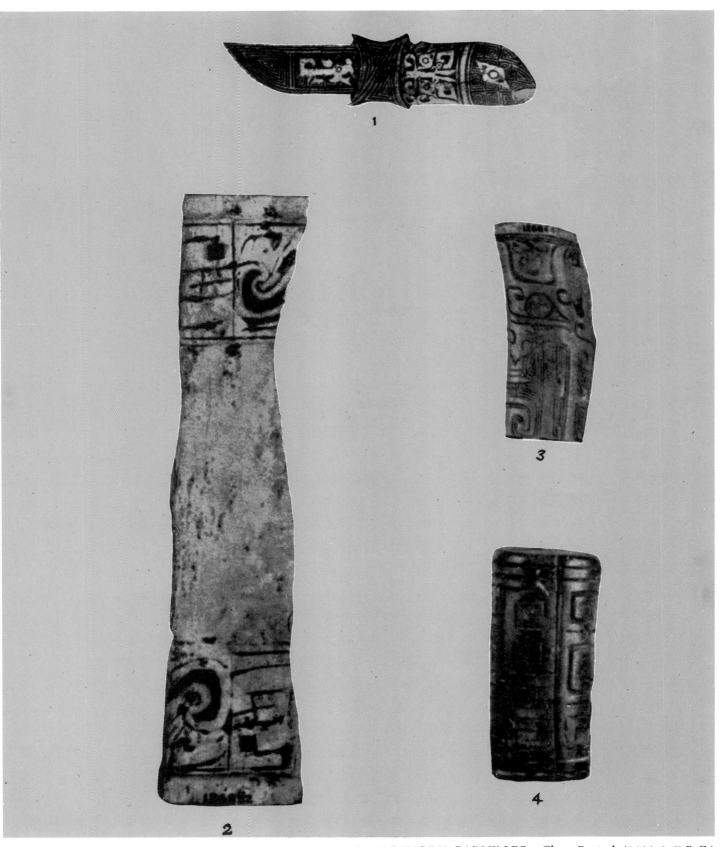

ARCHAIC IVORY CARVINGS—Chou Period (1122-247 B.C.)
1. Pick for untying a knot, a girdle ornament which symbolized
the ability to solve knotty problems. L. 4¼". *Metropolitan Museum of Art.* 2., 3. Knife handles. 4. Pommel of a knife. *Field Museum, Chicago.* Published by Berthold Laufer in "Ivory in China."

PLATE 2

This vessel is in the Louvre, or was before the war, and I illustrated it (Pl. XIV Bronze and Brass Ornamental Work in the 14th edition Encyclopaedia Britannica). Line drawings of two illustrated by Laufer and of this piece follow.

There are a number of authentic pre-Han ivory carvings known, some of which we show on Plate 2, reproduced from "Ivory in China' and belonging to the Field Museum, Chicago, having been brought in by the Capt. Marshall Field Expedition to China in 1923 except the first which belongs to the Metropolitan Museum of Art. This is an interesting example. It is an implement or point said to be used for "untying knots," and Laufer shows a similar one carved in jade (cf. "Jade", pp. 238-242) and says that they were symbolic of the ability to solve knotty problems, were worn suspended at the girdle as a token of maturity and of competence for the management of business. The design is obviously similar to those seen on bronzes showing an eye, a t'ao t'ieh head ("monster mask") and a running animal set off against a background of rectangular and triangular "cloud scroll" spirals. Whether or not the sagacity of the elephant lent further ideas to this form when it was rendered in ivory is not known. There is, so far as I know, nothing to confirm any idea of the Chinese that the elephant was a wise animal, although Ying Shao did write of the first tame elephant sent to the court of the Emperor Wu as I have said, "It quickly grasps man's intentions." Still this would hardly indicate that the animal was a solver of knotty problems and we must tentatively come to the conclusion that ivory was used as simply a valuable material without any special significance.

Two other picks for untying knots are from the Ralph M. Chait collection, one of which is unfortunately considerably eroded but interestingly suggests that these might have been made and used in pairs. The other is in perfect condition, though somewhat darkened as is to be expected with age

and it is the largest of these I have seen, larger also than jade examples which are of similar shape with an animal head at the top and tooth-like curved point below. Though the actual source of their discovery is not known, their style suggests that they surely are of the Shang to early Chou period and that they have likely come from An-yang. The curved groove down the center is not the result of a chip having broken off with the grain for on close inspection it is found to show curved tool-marks; it was done for some purpose and possibly to hold some sort of inlay.

The other objects on plate 2 consist of the handle and, in figure 4, the hilt or pommel of a knife found by Dr. Laufer himself in Peking in 1923. The designs on them are again unmistakably like those of contemporaneous bronzes.

It is said that some bows were tipped with ivory in early times but I have seen none of these pieces. Other objects such as pins and rings often unornamented are found and, in fact the chronicles have it that Confucius owned a ring "five inches wide," as Laufer says. Whether this was a *pi* disc or not he does not say. The chariots of state were also reportedly trimmed with ivory when of the third rank, the first being leather with jade trimming, the second leather with gold, the third leather with ivory, the fourth plain leather and the fifth plain wood in the Chou dynasty (1122-247 B.C.). The ceremonial leather cap worn by the emperors had a foundation of ivory at the back of the neck and was trimmed with various colored jade ornaments. There is no doubt, therefore, that it was considered a precious substance and when chopsticks were first made of ivory by the Emperor Chou, last of the Shang-Yin dynasty, a man of notorious debauchery, his relatives are said to have stated, "He makes chopsticks of ivory! Next he will doubtless make a cup of jade, finally he will think of the precious and extraordinary objects of distant countries, and will have them

IVORY HILT AND POMMEL—The ivory hilt and pommel showing turquoise inlay and design closely related to that of bronzes are of the Shang Dynasty (1783-1123 B.C.) and probably came from An-yang though actual data on their source is not known. *C. T. Loo & Co. Warren E. Cox Galleries.*

PLATE 3

SHANG IVORY HAIR PINS AND A WESTERN CHOU
BUCKLE—Typical of the Shang Dynasty (1783-1123 B.C.) are
these ceremonial hair-pins used in pairs and stained green to resemble jade. The bird-like odd one in the upper left hand corner
may be Late Shang to Early Chou. The buckle is of Western Chou,
and, it will be noted, has inlaid stones as well as incised decoration.
C. J. Loo & Co. Warren E. Cox Galleries.

PLATE 4

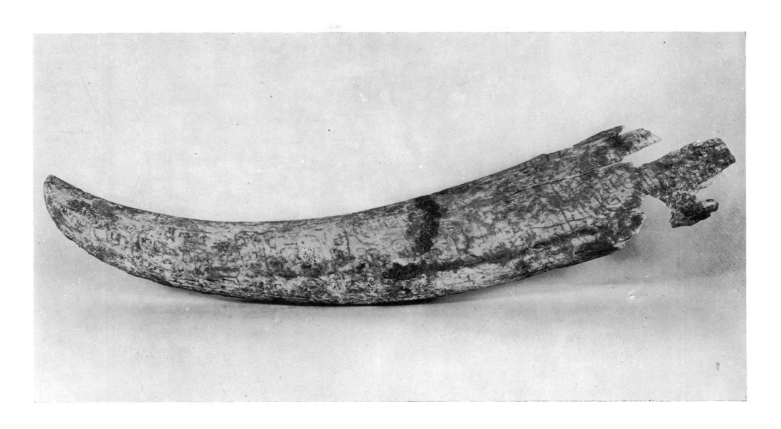

SHANG IVORY TUSK—This unique tip of a tusk engraved with decoration typical of the Shang period (1783-1123 A.D.) was found at An-yang and probably had a use similar to that of the better known engraved bones from that site. Length 19¼″.

IVORY BUCKLE—This ivory buckle with the interesting double shaft terminating in animal heads also undoubtedly had turquoise stones inlaid. It is of the Chou period. Length 6⅝″. *Both, G. L. Winthrop Bequest, The Fogg Museum of Art, Harvard University.*
PLATE 5

IVORY HU OR MEMORANDUM TABLET OF MING DY-
NASTY. *(Top)*—These memorandum tablets probably served a
practical purpose in the earlier times but came to be used as symbols of rank later on. This one is of the Ming Dynasty (1368-1644
A.D.). C. 18″. *Miss Ethelyn C. Stewart.*

SHANG IVORY TIGER. *(Bottom)*—Tiger forms like the above
are found both in jade and ivory. There are different characters in
Chinese writing for these and the memorandum tablets, but they
are both pronounced "hu." This piece is of the Shang Dynasty
(1783-1123 B.C.). L. 3⅛″. *C. T. Loo & Co. Warren E. Cox Galleries.*

PLATE 6

carted to his place. From that moment he will crave in ever increasing numbers chariots and horses, mansions and palaces, and there will be no way of keeping him off." (Translation given by Laufer, "Ivory in China" pp. 8-9) Little did they imagine that ivory chopsticks would be used by the hundreds in the restaurants of Chinatowns all over the world and that jade cups would be sold in many large sets for the drinking of cocktails by strangers three thousand years later!

Just as in the Near East ivory was used at very early times for sword furniture so the Chinese came to find this substance most suitable for sword-hilts and pommels such as those shown (Pl. 3), in the Shang period. The designs are, of course, closely related to those found on bronzes and, like the bronze ones, they seem also to have been inlayed with turquoise and other substances. Two outstandingly fine examples I illustrate from C. T. Loo & Co. and these are also included in our exhibition of 1945.

We are also privileged to show a group of the very rare hair-pins of Shang period. (Pl. 4) These probably had some ceremonial significance and are always found in pairs having been worn stuck in the knot of hair at the back of the head, one on either side. Some of them too, like the bird one in the upper left hand corner of our plate, may have had some inlay and also, they show signs of having been stained to resemble jade. It will be seen that the small buckle of Western Chou Dynasty has stones inlayed in it.

Scale armor and armor composed of small plates either in juxtaposition or overlapping like the scales of a fish was used in Assyria as is demonstrated by the monuments of King Sargon (722-705 B.C.). It probably originated in the reign of Salmanassar (860-825 B.C.) having come from Egypt where according to A. Erman (Life in Ancient Egypt p. 545, London 1894) a cuirass of thickly wadded material covered with metal plates was ascribed to the reign of Ramses II of the 13th century B.C. But evidence

is scant as to just when the idea was adopted by the Scythians and how it spread into China. Still more scant is any evidence as to when and where ivory plaques were so used though Dr. Walter Hough does speak of "hoop or band armor," (Primitive American Armor p. 633) saying, "This hoop armor is interesting as it shows the reproduction of plate armor types in skin, being made of horizontal bands of sealskin instead of rows of ivory plates, the rings telescoping together when the armor is not in use." Laufer further quotes Dr. Hough (Chinese Clay Figures p. 261), "In Eskimo armor made of five imbricating rows of plates of walrus ivory, lashing and adjustment of the plates is identical with certain types of Japanese armor." Later on page 266 Laufer says, "In the present state of our knowledge it is safe to assume that bone armor in northeastern Asia is as old as, or even older than, any iron plate armor in China or Korea," (Generally assumed to date from latter Han times) and continues, "If an outward impetus to the making of bone armor in that region must be assumed, I am disposed to believe that it came from the interior of Siberia." He then goes on to say, however, that we know very little about Siberian armor. There is one known rock carving found on the Yenisei River of Siberia which shows a mounted lancer clad in plate mail, but this has not been dated and the mail is thought to be of iron. Laufer thinks that this type of armor, being peculiarly adapted to fighting on horseback and the Iranian mode of tactics, was brought over the boundaries of Iran when such methods were used. However E. H. Minns (Scythians and Greeks, p. 188) shows five plates of bone of rectangular shape found in barrows about Popovka on the Sula River and in Southern Russia, which may be of earlier date than was at first supposed. So that we may tentatively think of this type of armor as having come into use in Northern China at least in Han times and possibly still earlier. This is borne out by two plates in Lau-

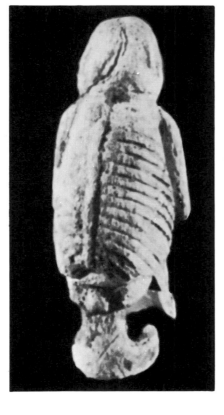

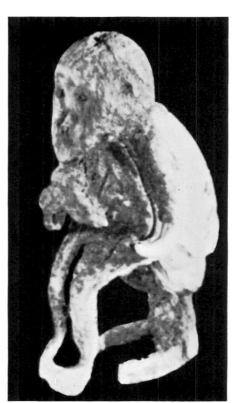

CHOU PERIOD IVORY MONKEY.—Carved from the point of a tusk, with the head and back of the outer layers and separated from the section composed of the legs and chest, this monkey is of the Chou Dynasty (1122-249 B.C.), probably of the Late Eastern Chou time (770-256 B.C.) and was probably a finial of some sort. *C. J. Loo & Co., Warren E. Cox Galleries.*

PLATE 7

fer's "Chinese Clay Figures" Pl. 15 and 16 clearly showing a jerkin of scales outlined in black, of which he says, "The lively fighting attitude and the body armor show us that the two shamans are engaged in a battle with the demons; and, if the tradition of the Chinese is correct that such clay figures were interred in the graves during the Chou period, we may infer that, as the shaman warded off pestilence and malignant spirits from the grave before the lowering into it of the coffin, he continued in this miniature form to act as the efficient guardian of the occupant of the grave." These figures were found in Honan Province and appear to me to be characteristic of the Han rather than the Chou period. He himself simply calls them of "Archaic Period." Therefore the evidence is not very strong unless we reason that such figures were likely to be traditional and that the shamans would probably not have worn the armor had it not existed in use for a fairly long time. However, that ivory was so used we can only guess until further evidence comes to light. It would naturally have come to hand far more easily in North Eastern China bordering the sea than in the north west. Yet Siberia has always been a source of both "dead ivory" and fossil ivory both mammoth and walrus and the speculation is interesting.

One other pre-Han use of ivory is interesting and that is that it was carved into "writing-tablets (*hu*)," as Laufer calls them (Ivory in China p. 8), for the use of the feudal princes. (Pl. 6) It was written that the Emperor himself used jade for this purpose. Laufer says that such tablets were rounded at the top and straight at the bottom to express the idea that the holder should obey the Son of Heaven. Later he tells us that those of the T'ang dynasty were of such shape while those of Ming dynasty were "angular at both ends." They were also made, he says, for great prefects, rounded at both bottom and top, "to express the idea that they had only superiors to obey," as he says, which is not quite clear. These tab-lets were often five or six times as long as they were broad and fairly thin being sometimes straight and sometimes slightly curved. They were suspended from the girdle and were used as memoranda pads or for jotting down notes. "An official, when he had an audience at court, inscribed his report on the tablet and recorded the emperor's reply or command. At later time they were reserved for the organs of government and became emblems of dignity." I illustrate one from the collection of Miss Ethelyn C. Stewart which measures 3¼ inches at the wide end and 2¼ inches at the narrow end which is slightly rounded. The length is 18 inches and the thickness tapers from about ¼ inch at the wide end to ⅛ inch at the narrow end. It is of beautiful quality ivory and dates back to Ming times. I do not know of an earlier available one in ivory.

It is evident that considerable confusion exists both in the minds of scholars and of the Chinese themselves concerning these tablets. Those with the points at the top are called "*kuei*" or according to Giles 6434, "A gem token conferred on feudal princes by the Emperor," while Una Pope-Hennessy says they are, "A narrow tablet with rectangular base and triangular point used in the worship of the East." The "*hu*" is according to Giles 4922, "A piece of jade cut in the shape of a tiger," and Una Pope-Hennesy adds, "A white jade emblem symbolizing or representing a tiger used in the worship of the West." The chinese characters for the memorandum tablet and the tiger are written differently but pronounced the same. We need not, however, go into this discussion here and I may add that I have never seen the pointed tablets rendered in ivory while most of those held in the hands of clay figures of the Six Dynasty or T'ang periods seem to taper slightly and to have straight or very slightly rounded tops. They are shown clasped by both hands before the body with the top coming to a little less than chin height. The figures holding them are always standing straight and with great dignity. Sometimes the clay figures have a slot made in the clasped hands and possibly the tablets were then of some other substance such as wood or actual ivory which has been lost or has rotted away in the tomb. This is born out by the round holes found in the hands of the warrior figures which probably held spears or even swords made of materials more suitable to their slender length than fired clay.

Thus we find that ivory was a valued and costly substance which the Chinese probably knew and worked as early or earlier than they knew bronze. We find it classed next to jade and gold in importance from a ritualistic viewpoint and we note that it was carved and worked with as great care. The elephant was well known to the ancient Chinese but they did little or no hunting of it and no domestication of it, leaving the hunting to outlying tribes and coming to domestication only by Han times (206 B.C.-220 A.D.). I must add that there is a record of one sort of use of the elephant for warfare. It was written that in 506 B.C. the prince of Ch'u launched against his enemy the king of Wu a herd of elephants with torches lighted and tied to their tails, but this would hardly have been done had the proper use of elephants in warfare been known and a trained herd would not have been so sacrificed.

By the end of the Chou period certainly at latest elephants had retreated to the Yangtse Valley from western Szechuan Province to the Eastern Coast and most of these were in the South West ranging from Kuantung and Hunan to Yunan as civilization progressed. The Chinese not having learned how to use the live elephant did not want him trampling around and an ancient saying from the *Tso chwan* of 548 B.C. states that the elephant has tusks which lead to the destruction of its body because they are used for gifts.

IV. Han, T'ang and Sung Periods

(c. 200 B.C. to 1350 A.D.)

THE HAN DYNASTY 206 B.C.-220 A.D.

WE have mentioned the first gift of a domesticated elephant from Nan Yüe to the Emperor Wu of the Han dynasty in 121 B.C. There is also a tradition to the effect that when the Emperor Shun Ti was buried in Ts'ang-wu in what would now be known as the Yung-chou prefecture, the Ning-yüan district in Hunan province, in 145 A.D. elephants trampled down the earth around his tumulus, so that the land looked like a ploughed field. This was the land of the Ch'u people who had made the gift of the elephant to Wu Ti and they were, according to Laufer, not Chinese but of the Tai stock and these people had for centuries domesticated elephants to a certain extent and kept them in the court of their king. Yet we have no Han period ivory carvings from them.

However, bronzes of the period of both north and south China have unmistakable elephant-head feet as have also the mortuary pottery wares in odd examples, and to quote Laufer, "In the monuments of the Han period there are highly naturalistic representations of the elephant in scenes carved on tomb sculptures," and he shows an outline drawing given below, which was taken from one of 8 stone slabs forming a part of a mortuary chamber found on the hill Hiao-t'ang-shan north west of Fei-ch'eng in western Shantung. This animal, he says, formed part of the retinue of a "barbarian" prince and though the elephant certainly did not exist in a wild state in this place at this time, he adds that there is little doubt but that it was drawn from life. But here again we find no examples of ivory carvings which can surely be attributed to Han.

Sowerby writes (Chinese Ivory Carving Ancient and Modern, China Journal Aug. 1934), "Many objects were made of ivory during the Han, Wei, Sui and T'ang Dynasties, but it must be admitted that this knowledge is derived from literary sources rather than from pieces that have survived to the present day. Indeed, T'ang carved ivory pieces are almost non-existent, while Sung pieces are exceedingly rare." Yet even these literary references are vague and more a source for speculation than actual proof of knowledge of ivory on the part of these people.

Fig. 16. PICTURE OF ELEPHANT AND MAHOUTS ON A BAS-RELIEF OF THE HAN DYNASTY (206 B.C.-220 A.D.)

From them we do know that in the central western part of the empire in what is now Szechuan province elephants were known to survive into Han times and were sent as tribute to the court of the emperors at Ch'ang-an where they were kept in a zoo. We also know that the people of what is now Yünnan province, the Tai who were the ancestors of the Siamese, made harness and helmets of elephant skin, and a Chinese expedition in the 2nd century B.C. to this country brought back reports of an "elephant riding" nation where the elephant was used in pageantry, as a riding animal, a draught animal and a

45

beast of burden. In 128 B.C. the Chinese received reports from Chang K'ien who went to Bactria and heard about the war-elephants of India, Persia and Cambodia. Nothing was written at this time of the mammoth or of mammoth ivory, and, if it was brought into China, it was not until much later that the Mongols and Manchus heard of an "ice rodent" from the Samoyeds. Thus there is a great hiatus in our chain of knowledge and, although I have searched high and wide, the only examples of Eastern Chou and Han periods I have been able to find are the charming combs from the C. T. Loo & Co. collection which we are illustrating and exhibiting (Pl. 8). Particularly the one mounted in gold is of great importance and shows how the material was valued.

Sowerby claims that the elephant was domesticated in T'ang times and shows for proof a pottery tomb-figure of one of these animals of that period which has on it some sort of saddle-cloth and trappings. The figure belonged to Peter J. Bahr and, therefore, I do not doubt its proper attribution, but again pure logic indicates that there were many other possibilities which might have brought it into being, particularly when one remembers the many foreign motives introduced into T'ang art. One might as well argue that the Chinese had big noses because figures of T'ang pottery are found with distinctly semitic profiles, or, for that matter, that dinosaurs existed because the Weis made reconstructions of them imagined from their bones found lying *en situ* (See Pottery & Porcelain pp. 93-98 in which I advance the theory.).

He also believes that as late as Han times elephants were as far north as the Yangtze in outlying, wooded sections in a wild state, and this might possibly be true, though they could not have been in any appreciable number in the north eastern part of this section, as we have made clear, and during Han times they became extinct except for the imported ones

46

kept in zoological gardens of the emperors who had a lively curiosity concerning strange animals and plants from distant lands.

T'ANG AND LATER PERIODS
(618 to 906 and later)

In the south in Kuangtung province it was a different matter and the records tell us that in the 7th century in T'ang times the animal was still plentiful in Tonking and in the prefectures of Ch'ao-chou, Hui-chou and Lei-chou where it was hunted for its flesh which the natives regarded as a delicacy. The trunk was considered the best part, possibly not entirely because of its taste but because of some vague ideas of magic associated with it. The tusks of this Kuangtung elephant were described as small but of a warm "reddish" color very suitable for ivory tablets or hu. The Chinese also say that this southern elephant was black while the white elephants came from India and Syria "Fu-lin". Two of these rare animals are also recorded: One sent from Gandhara in 509 A.D. and kept near the capitol, Loyang, in Honan province, and the other sent from Burma to Hui Tsung, the Sung emperor in 1105 A.D. The records also tell us that up to the 10th century elephants were used in Canton in putting criminals to death. Laufer quotes from the Memoirs of Chou Ta-kwan, who visited Cambodia in 1295-97 (Yüan period, 1280-1368 A.D.) as follows, "The ivory from the tusk of an elephant killed by means of a pike is considered best; next in quality is the ivory of an animal which was found shortly after it died a natural death, while least esteemed is that discovered in mountains many years after the animal's death." Similar references are found in the Chinese materia medica even up to the present day and always the "live ivory," is considered best. It was also noted that "dead ivory" is always covered with opaque, brown spots of various sizes. Dr. Laufer says that the Chinese thought that

EASTERN CHOU AND HAN COMBS OF IVORY AND GOLD—The beautiful combs shown above are of Eastern Chou and Han periods. Most interesting is the careful sawing of the lower left one with a repoussé gold back and the staining of them green to resemble jade in many instances. The top center one might almost be thought of as Egyptian in design. *C. T. Loo & Co. Warren E. Cox Galleries.*

PLATE 8

EARLY T'ANG IVORY FIGURE. *(Left)*—I have never seen another figure in ivory like this. It is quite similar, though not in scale, to the pottery ones of the period and has great charm though the one arm is missing. Ht. 1¹¹⁄₁₆″. *Courtesy of Langdon Warner, Cambridge, Mass.*

Exceedingly rare T'ang ivory figure with polychrome decoration *(right)*. Ht. 8¾″. *Fogg Museum of Art. Ex Winthrop collection.*
PLATE 9

the elephant shed its tusks and hid them in a hole dug for this purpose, and, if they were taken away, it was best to leave a pair of wooden teeth in their place so the animal would not notice the theft. They also thought that the designs in the grain of elephant ivory were formed when the animal was frightened by thunder, just as they thought that the patterns of rhinoceros horn were formed when the animal gazed at the moon.

SUNG PERIOD (960 to 1280)

Fan Cho wrote an account of a visit to Yünnan in 860 and in it said that the natives used elephants to draw their ploughs. Thus a common knowledge of the sources of ivory was built up through the T'ang and Sung dynasties, but I think the first reference to African ivory is that in the *Ling wai tai ta* written by Chou K'ü-fei in 1178 in which he refers to it as "great ivory." However, the Arab geographer Masudi states in 983 A.D. that Arabic ships brought the ivory of the "Zenj", as negroes were called, into Oman on the east coast of Arabia and thence to India and China. Laufer says he further states that the tusks were straight or but slightly curved and were held in high esteem by the Chinese and were used for the making of palanquins for persons of high rank. By the 12th century the Chinese had fully recognized the better quality of African ivory and wrote of tusks that weighed over 100 pounds.

Rare as actual T'ang ivories are I am fortunate in being able to show illustrations of two examples. (See Pl. 9) The first is a miniature figure of a typical T'ang dancing girl in graceful pose with long sleeve uplifted. It is a tiny thing only about an inch and a half high but full of life. This was also very kindly lent me for the exhibition by Mr. Langdon Warner of the Fogg Museum of Art, Cambridge. I am also indebted to Mr. Warner for the photograph of another figure which belongs to the Winthrop Collec-

tion in the same museum. This figure, about 7 inches tall, was carved from the tip of a tusk and the artist very cleverly arranged the arms to carry out the pointed form. It is not so alive as the miniature one but is a fine piece of carving nevertheless and the robe is colored in deep tones of red and green. So nearly is it styled like the well known pottery examples that there can be no doubt of its attribution as of the T'ang dynasty, but the colors, as was the case with many wood carvings, have probably been touched up several times. I should like to be able to investigate these closely to see if there are more ancient layers of colors underneath. Both of these examples are the rarest of the rare and I know of no others of the period.

Thus we know that the Sung dynasty Chinese did get some ivory and knew where it came from but with the excellent markets of the Near East and of India nearer at hand it is probable that the Arab ships only occasionally brought ivory to China and the trade was sporadic, not furnishing enough material so that many artists could devote their entire lives to the carving of it, as became possible later. Specimens are very rare but I feel that we can advance with some assurance the three which I illustrate herewith, from the Metropolitan Museum of Art, as late Sung (Pl. 10). The attribution is not based upon facts but is the result of comparisons with wood carvings of the period. These three beautiful figures (one unfortunately headless) represent in the center Sâkyamuni or Gautama, the last earthly incarnation of Buddha, with right side of the breast bare, with the *ushnisha* (protuberances on the front of the skull of a Buddha), the *urna* (mark in the center of the forehead), the curly hair and the long ear lobes. He is seated in the *padmasana mudra* or posture, cross legged on a lotus throne with right hand raised to shoulder height, palm outward and fingers pointed upward except for the third one which touches the tip of the thumb in the *mudra* or hand posture known as *vitarka*, that of exposition or argument. The Buddha is seated on a ch'i lin, the fabulous creature with head of a dragon with flame about it, the body being the shape of a deer but covered with scales and the tail flaring, for this animal represents happiness and perfection and is supposed to foreshadow the coming of a great ruler. It is admittedly not a Buddhistic animal but the material, style and surface seem to prove that it belongs to this group and it should certainly, therefore be placed between the earthly animals, the lion and the elephant. If this be true the figures to left and right are Manjusri or Wen Shu the god of thought and wisdom (headless) on the lion, and Samantabhadra or P'u Hsien, the all wise one, to the Buddha's right on the elephant. Both hold the *utpala* or blue lotus. (See p. cxliv "Chinese Sculpture" by Oswald Sirén.) Of course the head of the flower in the hands of Wen Shu is also unfortunately missing.

The ivory of which these figures is carved has become quite dark with age and it is interesting to note that traces of contemporary polychrome remain. Thus even at this early date the receptive surface continued to attract the colorist. Possibly the treatment of woods also had an effect for it was not until Ming times that we find the great flood of monochrome, lacquered wood figures, and not until Ming times that many ivory figures seem to have been made without coloring. The alive, expressive and yet delicate carving of these three figures is surely that of a great artist who knew his medium and pressed its advantages in obtaining far more detail than is ever found in wood sculptures.

The general question of polychrome decoration of ivory is an interesting one. We know, of course, that many of the earliest stone carvings had applications of color on them. There is ample evidence bronzes of Chou and Shang-Yin times had inlays of turquoise and, at times probably red or black pigment in the grooves of the castings. Therefore, it is

quite understandable that the beautiful surface of ivory, so smooth and light in tone would immediately suggest itself as a ground for color, and this would become even more enticing when it was found that ivory is readily receptive of transparent stains which allow the beautiful grain of the material to remain visible. Actually the Chinese did start staining ivory carvings in Shang-Yin times as is proven by some of the pairs of hair-pins and some combs found at An-yang. Blue and green seemed to have been favorite colors and were probably copper derivatives. A beautiful semi-circular comb, curved at the back and with teeth meeting the flat edge, is bound around the whole curved edge with beautifully detailed pressed gold. The piece is cut from a section of tusk like a slab of cheese with the back edge about half an inch thick and the straight edge thin, giving a natural taper to the teeth. (Pl. 8.) Another comb of almost Egyptian appearance has a flat top surmounted by two animals, concave sides and flaring tooth section. This has been stained a beautiful turquoise color. Thus we see that even in Shang and Chou times color was used to enhance the beauty of the material. (See Pl. 8.)

Later in Ming times we shall see that the style changed to more baroque carving which was often, though not always, left without color additions.

The dearth of material in what may be called these middle Chinese periods was undoubtedly due directly to the retreat of the elephant from the northern half of the country while trade from Siam, India and Africa was not well enough established to provide a continuous supply of ivory.

The memorandum tablets which we described were also made in T'ang times and are said by Laufer to be rounded above and angular below. (See p. 73 "Ivory in China"). This is borne out by the ones represented in the hands of pottery figures. (See Pl. 30, "Pottery and Porcelain" by the author.)

The Japanese Treasure House at Nara is said to

THREE LATE SUNG IVORY CARVINGS—Three spiritual and beautiful carvings of Buddha, center, Wen Shu, headless and on the lion, and P'u Hsien, on the elephant. Hts. c. 9″. *Metropolitan Museum of Art.*

PLATE 10

contain a backgammon board of sandalwood inlaid in ivory and of the T'ang period, and two standard "foot-measures" of ivory of the same period and stained red and green. Omura Seigai writes that ivory of the 8th century was stained green, indigo, crimson and other colors with flowers in the natural color of the ivory and engraved. Possibly the batik process was used. (See "Batik", in Encyclopaedia Britannica 14th edition, by the author.) Laufer also says, "The fact that ivory was painted in China under the T'ang may be gleaned from an ivory fragment found by Sir Aurel Stein (Serindia, p. 779) in the Limes of Tun-hwang; it bears traces of a painted leaf-scroll in green. Ivory dyed by means of purple in Asia Minor was known in the Homeric age (Iliad, IV, 141). The Hawaiians colored whale ivory yellow by smoking it with green banana leaves."

V. Ming Ivories

(c. 1368 to 1644)

IT IS strange that the Ming dynasty was a period in which porcelain began to be decorated with many colors while ivory carvings were largely left untouched but this seems to be the case. It is even more strange that most Ming ivory carvings show no trace of having been lacquered for lacquering was extensively used on wood carvings. The stone carvings were usually also undisguised and possibly the only explanation is that the artists so appreciated the natural textures of polished stone and polished ivory that they purposely left them alone. Later in the last part of the 17th century and during the 18th century the art of lacquering on ivory, and of painting it, was revived with such good taste that the material loses none of its richness and where exposed seems actually more precious and beautiful. Only small decorative pieces of Ming ivory are ever colored. At the close of the Sung period in 1280 the Mongols had completed the conquest started in 1127. Kublai Khan (1214-1294 A.D.) the grandson of Genghis Khan, the great conqueror, was sovereign over China and much of the Far East and he was famed for having a large herd of elephants in his possession, some 200 of which were captured by the Mongols from the Burmese in 1277. Marco Polo tells us that the Burmese had 2000 elephants, "on each of which was set a tower of timber, well framed and strong, and carrying from 12 to 16 well-armed fighting men," but these elephants could not stand the hail of Mongol arrows, any better than could the armored knights of Europe, and turned tail and ran. Marco Polo later tells us that the great Khan had some 5000 elephants which were especially shown, wonderfully caparisoned, and carrying

the silver plate and furniture for the New Year's Festival. He also says that they were used on hunting expeditions and that four were trained to carry a fine chamber made of timber and lined with plates of beaten gold for the Khan. Live elephants, we are told by Laufer, were taken to Samarkand and Khotan and thence marched overland to China, and right up to the reign of Ch'ien Lung (1736-1796), they were sought after and kept by the emperors. He says of this emperor, "on the evening before the winter solstice, he proceeded to the Altar of Heaven to offer sacrifice at dead of night, and he mounted a carriage drawn by an elephant."

Laufer again interestingly quotes E. Ysbrants Ides, envoy to the Emperor K'ang Hsi (1672-1722) in the years of 1692-95 as follows: "The emperor's life-guards were clothed in red calico, printed with red figures, and wore small hats with yellow feathers. They were armed with scimitars and lances. There were eight white saddle-horses for show. In the third court of state were four extraordinarily large elephants, one of which was white. They were all covered with richly embroidered cloth, and their trappings were ornamented with silver gilt. On their backs was a finely carved wooden castle spacious enough for eight persons. Being taken out of the court, I mounted one of the emperor's two-wheeled carts, and was drawn to my apartment by an elephant. There were ten persons on each side with a rope in their hands fastened to the elephant's mouth to lead him; and on his neck sat a man with an iron hook to guide him. He walked at his ordinary rate of speed, but this obliged the men to run, in order to keep up with him. In the emperor's stables there were fourteen elephants: they made them roar, sing like a canary, neigh, blow a trumpet, go down on their knees, etc. All these elephants were extraordinarily large, and the teeth of some a full fathom long. The mandarins told me that the King of Siam annually sends several by way of tribute." But even this use of elephants grew less and less for Laufer quotes John Bell of Antermony who observed in Peking in 1721, the year before the end of the K'ang Hsi reign, "After dinner we saw the huge elephants richly caparisoned in gold and silver stuffs. Each had a driver. We stood about an hour admiring these sagacious animals, who, passing before us at equal distances, returned again behind the stables, and so on, round and round, till there seemed to be no end of the procession. The plot, however, was discovered by the features and dress of the riders: the chief keeper told us there were only sixty of them. The emperor keeps them only for show, and makes no use of them, at least in these northern parts. Some of them knelt and made obeisance to us; others sucked up water from vessels, and spouted it through their trunks among the mob, or wherever the driver directed."

The Earl of Macartney in 1792 toward the end of the reign of Ch'ien Lung (1736-1796) said he saw elephants in the imperial palace which were brought from "the neighborhood of the equator" and bred, "to the northward of the Tropic." He said the Chinese elephants were smaller and lighter in hue than the Cochin-China ones and lived on rice and millet. Later in 1834 in the description of Peking in the *Chinese Repository* it was said that not more than eight or ten elephants were kept in the Siang Fang ("Elephant's Palace"), and finally Dr. Laufer tells us that he himself visited the building in 1901 and there were no more elephants there.

Even when large herds of elephants were kept by the emperors, they were, of course, no source of ivory and it was undoubtedly supplied some as trib-

ute from Indonesia, and some from trade with the Arabs and other foreigners who brought in African ivory. Of mammoth ivory Laufer tells us that in the *Shen i king*, a book of stories attributed to Tung-fang So, minister to emperor Wu (140-87 B.C.) of the Han Dynasty, there is this passage, "In the regions of the north, where ice is piled up over a stretch of country ten thousand miles long and reaches a thickness of a thousand feet, there is a rodent called *k'i shu*, living beneath the ice in the interior of the interior of the earth. In shape it is like a rodent, and subsists on herbs and trees. Its flesh weighs a thousand pounds and may be used as dried meat for food; it is eaten to cool the body. Its hair is about eight feet in length, and is made into rugs, which are used as bedding and keep out the cold. The hide of the animal yields a covering for drums, the sound of which is audible over a distance of a thousand miles. Its hair is bound to attract rats. Wherever its hair is found rats will flock together." Tall as this tale is it had some reason, for it was true that the animal was always found frozen in the ice or ground and, if one of our modern scientists could have been present to tell the writer the actual facts concerning the mammoth, he would have been thought a liar or spinner of taller tales. It was also referred to as *fen*, a species of mole, but the striking thing is that these early accounts do not make any allusion to the tusks, although the Chinese materia medica refers to "dragon's bones" and "dragon's teeth" and the former have been sold right up to today and were proven in some cases to be fossil ivory by the microscopic investigations of D. Hanbury (Science Papers, p. 273).

In 1712-15 the Manchu, Tulishen, writes in his Memoirs much the same description as that given above and associates the animal definitely with the mammoth, and in 1716 the emperor K'ang Hsi wrote of the permanent ice and the *Yuan kien lei han* contains the following statement, "The *k'i shu*, which is described as reaching the weight of ten thousand pounds, is found even at the present day." (Of course this was not so if he meant alive.) "In shape it resembles an elephant and its tusks are like those of the same beast, but the ivory is yellowish in color." . . . Thus it is evident that although the Chinese did at times get some fossil ivory which they used as medicine, they knew little about its source even in the 18th century, and it stands to reason that little was used for carvings.

Walrus ivory was first known in China in T'ang times (618-906) and was called *ku-tu kio* and some was received as tribute from the Kitan and other Tungusian tribes. (See Walrus Ivory In China, Berthold Laufer, p. 53) In 1090-1155 Hung Hao wrote in his memoirs *Sung mo ki wen,* "The *ku-tu* horn is not very large. It is veined like ivory and is yellow in color. It is made into sword-hilts, and is a priceless jewel." Chou Mi (1230-1320) wrote, "*ku-tu* is a horn of the earth," and again, "*ku-tu-si* is the horn of a large snake and that, being poisonous by nature, it is capable of counteracting all poisons, as poison is treated with poison." Ye Sen (These are all from the same source, "Walrus Ivory in China") wrote that knife-hilts of *ku-tu-si* resembled the sugar-cakes sold in the markets and had white spots like those on candied pastry. He also said, "When touching this substance with your hands it emits an odor like that of cinnamon; when after rubbing it no odor is perceptible, it is a counterfeit." This was in 1320 so walrus ivory was well enough known and used to have already been counterfeited. Finally Laufer says, "Toward the latter part of the 17th century, when the Russians established commercial relations with China, they traded chiefly two articles—seal-skins and walrus tusks, the latter being styled in the Russian documents of the time 'bones of walrus tooth.' " In the beginning of the 18th century the *Cheng tse t'ung* speaks of a, "fish or seal with teeth as strong and bright as bone and adorned with designs as fine as silk,—workable into implements." And in the 19th century Americans brought "hai-ma ya" or "sea horse teeth," to China.

Thus it is understandable that ivory in China has always been a most precious substance and we now know why even Ming carvings are scarce and valuable. Let us examine some of those shown by the author in his gallery in the large exhibition of some 300 pieces of all periods in November 1945, and also those illustrated in various works on the subject, taking the latter first.

In his excellent work *"Ivory in China"* by Berthold Laufer, which we have often quoted, there are two examples of Ming ivory only (See Pl. 11). The first and larger one is a Kwan Yin, a favorite subject for the ivory carvers as we shall see, and possibly not only because of the general popularity of this deity but also because, having now become entirely female, the flowing line of her robes and graceful pose seem to fit perfectly the curve of the tusk and the delicacy of the medium. In this rendering she holds a bowl in her left hand. This is believed to be filled with the nectar of immortality. Her right hand touches a ladle ready to distribute the nectar to her devotees. The other figure is of Tung-fang So whom we met as the author of a book of marvels, the *Shen i king,* and minister to the Han Emperor Wu. He lived in the 2nd century B.C. and was an adept versed in the mysteries of Taoism. He was possessed of supernatural powers and divine wisdom and is said to have thrice abstracted from paradise the peaches of immortality which ripen but once in three years. He was called The Wit. In his hand he holds a fan.

The colors of these figures are dark brown and deep brownish yellow. It will be noted in each of these figures that the artist has beautifully adapted his design to the medium. Although they are of such diameter that they could have been carried out along straight lines, they have purposely been curved to suggest the curve of the tusk, and large areas are left

TWO MING CARVINGS.—1. Kwan Yin of the full faced type holding a bowl. 2. Shen i king the minister to the Han Emperor Wu. Hts. c. 11½″ & 9″. *Field Museum, Chicago. Capt. Marshall Field Expedition.*

BUDDHIST MONK.—The simple treatment of this figure almost surely places it in the Ming Dynasty although the museum calls it "K'ang Hsi." Ht. 10″. *Metropolitan Museum of Art*

PLATE 11

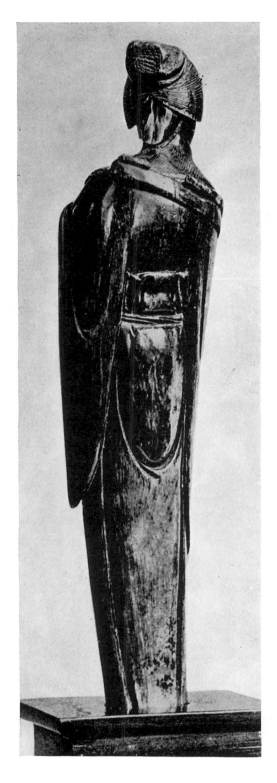

BACK OF IVORY FIGURE FROM THE LION COLLECTION, PARIS. *(Left)*—Note the simple conventionalization which leaves broad spaces in which the texture of the material shows well. Ht. 7⅞".

MING IVORY LADY WITH THE PEACHES OF IMMORTALITY. *(Center)*—This typical Ming ivory (1368-1644 A.D.) shows the portrait, life-like quality which was obtained and the slight sway to the body carrying out the curve of the tusk. Ht. 7¼". *Ralph Dudley Col., Warren E. Cox Galleries.*

BACK OF THE SAME FIGURE OF MING IVORY LADY. *(Right)*—It is interesting to compare the backs of the two figures shown to see how very closely the conventions were followed. Note the break in the U fold of the skirt, the similar treatments of the sleeves and the slant of the collar, as well as the hair arrangement.

PLATE 12

MING IVORY CARVING. *(Top, left)*—The museum calls this a figure of Kwan Yin although it has strong portrait-like qualities. Ht. 5⅜″. *Metropolitan Museum of Art.*

PORTRAIT IN IVORY. *(Top, right)*—Quite probably a portrait of an official of the Ming period and showing some traces of lacquer, this figure is well designed and compact while having at the same time a life-like expression. Ht. 5½″. *C. T. Loo & Co.*

PORTRAIT OF A DUTCH LADY. *(Bottom, left)*—This is probably a portrait of some actual Dutch lady in 16th century costume. Yet it is not unique for I have seen one other very much like it. Ming (c. 1600). Ht. 7½″. *Ralph Dudley Col., Warren E. Cox Galleries.*

CHAN-TS'AI-TONG-TSEU. *(Bottom, right)* — The figure of Chan-Ts'ai-Tong-Tseu, though conventional in attitude and general treatment, often shows a portrait-like expression. Ht. 7″.

PLATE 13

on each quite plain so that the beauty of the grain can be enjoyed. Although this is not always the case with Ming ivories a great many of them are so conceived as will be seen in similar examples shown on plate No. 12 from the Ralph Dudley Collection and exhibited. Even the seated figures such as that shown from the C. T. Loo collection, which is probably a portrait of an official (Pl. 13), are treated with simple, broad lines of the robe so that large areas of the plain surface of the material are exposed unhampered by ornamentation. Alan Priest claims that portraits were done, "There are precedents for sculptured portraits—a bronze now owned by Mrs. Yale Kneeland, N. Y., was certainly intended to represent Huan I, an official; and on anonymous loan in the Museum is a small figure of an official, which Chinese scholars maintain is a Sung figure used as an ancestor portrait." But he does not tell us how or why the one is so certain, nor does he state who the "Chinese scholars," are. In any event a comparison between the ivory ones and the wood example is much to the benefit of the former. Note the example from Metropolitan Museum along with Mr. Loo's. (Pl. 13—No. 1 and No. 2) They are simple, yet expressive of personality in such a way that they may well be portraits. They are not tricked out with extra ornamentation and real hair beards such as were added to wood examples, and age has enhanced the beauty of the material, instead of breaking down the surface, because it was left unpainted and unlacquered. They have become works of art which one's hand almost instinctively reaches out for, to touch, to turn over and to examine more closely, while the wood ones are fragile, and chipped, and rusty in color. The ivory has tactile appeal and the artists who carved it foresaw this and made their designs compact and without unnecessary projections often found in late Ming wood carving.

In the interesting catalogue of the Lion Collection of Paris ("Les Ivoires Religieux et Médicaux" by Henri Maspero, René Grousset and Lucien Lion) there is an arresting observation to the effect that there are really three quite different conceptions of Kwan-Yin: 1.—Those with long oval faces, the long ears of Buddhist figures, smooth hair and the expression of purity and spirituality seldom seen elsewhere, (see Pl. 20) 2.—Those of more Asiatic aspect, with head more voluminous, body more robust and more sensual lips; the attitude the same in general but a more "heathen goddess," (Pl. 11 and 20) (Both of these are standing.) and 3.—The seated figures with one leg folded and one pendant, richly garbed, with finely carved diadems and looking "like a princess from the Arabian Nights; a real Sultana." (Pl. 14) The suggestion is made that perhaps these come from different parts of China; the spiritual types from the north and the more earthly from the south, but there is no conclusive evidence and it will be seen in the examples from the Hough Collection that both the spiritual and queenly types were carved later in Peking. This theory hardly holds water, too, because there is no sign of the southern love for ornamental detail so typical of the Canton craftsmanship in the figures with fuller faces (See Pl. 11 Fig. 1 which Laufer shows). Possibly the differences simply occur in the different personal conceptions of the carvers and this seems borne out by the fact that a single figure may represent at least two of the types having well defined characteristics of both. Thus the one just mentioned is both full of face and of "Asiatic aspect" and also highly spiritual etc., and the Kwan-Yin shown from the Lion collection with "Long-Wang-Niu", the "daughter of the Dragon King" and "Chan-Ts'ai-Tong-Tseu," the young man of "capacities excelentes," as the book describes them, is both representative of type 3 and of type 2. (Pl. 15) If we were to venture a guess, it might be that the three types are more likely to represent differences in period; the first period of Early Ming comprising the rounded faced, "Asiatic" or Mongol

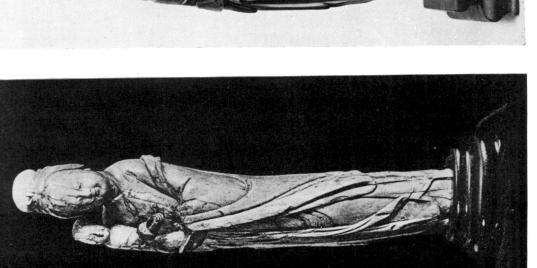

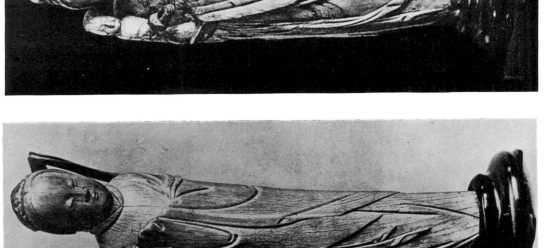

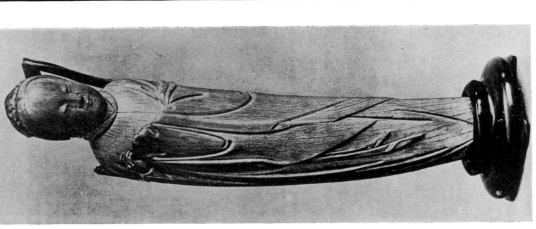

Two figures (left) of Kwan-Yin of the 2nd type with full faces and strongly Asiatic aspect. Both are Ming. Hts. 10⅜" and 8⅝". *Lion Col. France.*

Kwan Yin of the full faced type (No. 3) and of the Ming period, though called by the museum "K'ang Hsi." Ht. 10½". *Metropolitan Museum of Art.*

And (right) a remarkable ivory carving of Kwan-yin made in the Ming Dynasty and greatly resembling certain gothic types of madonnas. This is representative of the queenly type No. 3. Ht. 4⅜". *Lion Col. France.*

PLATE 14

THREE BUDDHISTIC FIGURES—Ming ivory carving of Kwan-Yin with Long-Wang-Niu, the daughter of the Dragon King, and Chan-Ts'ai-Tong Tseu, the excellent young man. Hts. 5¾" and 3⅜". *Lion Coll.*

PLATE 15

type No. 2 (See dated wood Pl. CXVII Chinese Sculpture in the Metropolitan Museum, dated 1385), the second type the more spiritual, oval faced ones of the No. 1 group, and the Late Ming or 17th century ones more ornate though each period has its throwbacks. However, this judging of style is a very delicate matter in Chinese art and there are many wide differences of opinion. Thus some Sung sculpture and, of course, T'ang as well, is very ornate and some 18th century figures, and even later ones, are full of the highest spiritual qualities. We also find representations of Tung-fang So, the old man with fan in hand which seem to be Ming, K'ang Hsi, Chien Lung and later, but very similar in style only to be distinguished by the color and condition of the ivory. It is well to take with a grain of salt the words of those who are very sure about such things unless some circumstantial evidence is offered.

In any event some of the finest sculpture in the world is found in the Ming Dynasty, a time much scorned by some "experts", and in ivory, a medium highly neglected by most writers on sculpture. To quote from "Les Ivoires Religieux et Médicaux" the passage translated from the great French historian M. Maurice Paléologue," The beautiful ivories denote work that is honest, energetic and firm, a carving without hesitation sharp cut. The tight tissue of the material is attacked vigorously, cut with brief contours and numerous faces where the light glides, and is reflected. This method does not exclude large and supple accents. Certain pieces owe precisely their seduction to the softness of their modelling."

Another interesting Ming carving from the C. T. Loo collection is a boy with drum, seated upon a stupa-like base. (Pl. 16) The Field Museum has an ivory seal in the form of a tope or stupa and Laufer says that such seals were used by Buddhist monks. This one has a design of the cat on it for the cat was made sacred for exterminating the rats which threatened the sacred books with destruction. Laufer says

the domestic cat was introduced into China by the Buddhists and spread to the whole Far East. The Ralph Dudley collection has a most wonderful small base probably designed to hold a smoky crystal ball. It consists of four lions, one might say *very* rampant, standing on their hind legs and pushing upward with muscles bulging. It is a tiny thing but bursting with power. Also in our exhibition is a large and wonderful lion from the Ralph M. Chait collection carved with directness and full of life. This animal, called "*Shih*" in Chinese, has large, round eyes, a short nose and one is in no doubt that, though by nature it is ferocious, its present mood is one of gentleness. Its paw holds the sacred streamer attached to the mystical brocaded ball or "*chu*". On the back a square opening indicates that upon it was a figure undoubtedly of Manjusrî or as the Chinese call him Wen-shu who is the apotheosis of transcendental wisdom. (See description of three Sung figures at Metropolitan Museum of Art Pl. 10.) One wonders what a magnificent figure this must have been, and dreams of another group of three of which it might possibly have been a part, for the lion is a great work of art. Still another figure which belongs to Mr. Chait is that of a Chinese wearing a turban of the style used in Western China and Turkestan. (Pl. 17)

Again from Turkestan probably comes this figure of a mourner dressed in rich robes which appear to be fur lined and holding in his sobs with his sleeve. Both he and the supplicating priest could hardly be more simple in rendering yet more filled with emotion. These I consider two of the finest pieces from the Lion Collection of Paris. The best of the Renaissance in Europe shows us nothing better than these pieces and they are truly great art and rare treasures.

Other things were made, brush-holders (*pi tung* or *pi ch'ung*) (Pl. 41), table screens and wrist rests (Pl. 18) for the scholar's table, brushes with ivory handles and sheaths, and measures etched in

62

black with delicate floral designs and birds in color, but these things are rarely of the Ming period. Laufer shows a "desk ornament" which looks like a rough rock that might be used in a garden and says it is possibly a piece of mammoth ivory left in its natural state, being only sawed off and polished. Of walrus ivory he says that back-scratchers, handles for fans, chop-sticks, ear-rings, dice and small ornaments were made and often dyed green with verdigris. Which of these are Ming and which later it is hard to tell. He does show one small dish of walrus ivory carved into a swirl of waves rising to crests along the edge which might well be Ming. It too is stained green.

Laufer also tells us that under the Mongols in the Yüan dynasty (1260-1367 A.D.) a bureau was set up for the carving of ivory and rhinoceros-horn, and that in it couches, tables, implements and girdle-ornaments inlaid with ivory were turned out. He says that in 1263 an official was put in charge and some hundred and fifty workmen were employed. We also know that later toward the end of the 17th century K'ang Hsi had a similar establishment but more about that later.

In Ming times the ivory tablets (*hu*) were angular at both ends and Laufer says they were granted to officials above the fourth grade; "those of the fifth grade and below had wooden ones with painted designs." He goes on to say that they were abolished under the Manchu but were used in Korea down to recent times. Yüan Shi-kai, he says, tried to revive them toward the end of his presidency as part of his effort to revive the monarchy, but failed. The example, already mentioned, and which belongs to Miss Ethelyn C. Stewart, is a typical Ming one. (See Pl. 6) Of these Friar William Rubruck who was with the Mongol court from 1253 to 1255 is quoted by Laufer, "Whenever the principal envoy came to court, he carried a highly polished tablet of ivory about a cubit long and half a palm wide. Every time he spoke to the Khan or some great personage, he always looked at the tablet as if he found there what he had to say, nor did he look to the right or to the left, nor in the face of him with whom he was talking. Likewise, when coming into the presence of the Lord, and when leaving it, he never looked at anything but his tablet."

Unfortunately none of these figures or objects are signed by the artists who made them. No names of famous ivory-carvers are known so that we have no information as to schools of styles in the various parts of the country and at various times. It is amazing that those who worked in this precious substance with such very great mastery should have been lost to posterity but that unfortunately is the case, and the same thing is largely true of all the crafts; few names of potters, of makers of bronze, jewelers or other artists, save those of painters, have come down to us.

POWERFUL LION IVORY CARVING—This wonderful animal was probably a base for a figure of Wen-shu and is full of the finest baroque vigor to be seen in any art of the East or West. Length c. 7". *Ralph M. Chait Col., Warren E. Cox Galleries.*

BOY WITH DRUM — This Ming carving of a happy boy with drum is mounted on a stupa-like base which is not, however, a seal as is sometimes the case. Note the beautiful texture that time has given the piece. Ht. 5¼". *C. J. Loo & Co. Warren E. Cox Galleries.*

STAND FOR A CRYSTAL BALL. (*Right*)—Little of the finest art of the baroque can equal this powerful bit of Ming ivory carving. (Two views.) The color is dark brown to light amber. Ht. 2½". *Ralph Dudley Col., Warren E. Cox Galleries.*

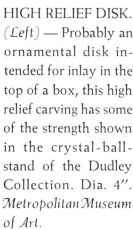
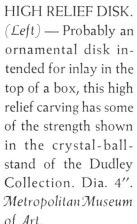

HIGH RELIEF DISK. (*Left*) — Probably an ornamental disk intended for inlay in the top of a box, this high relief carving has some of the strength shown in the crystal-ball-stand of the Dudley Collection. Dia. 4". *Metropolitan Museum of Art.*

PLATE 16

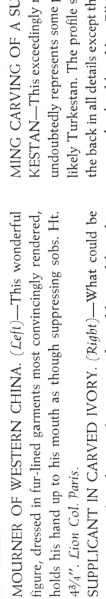

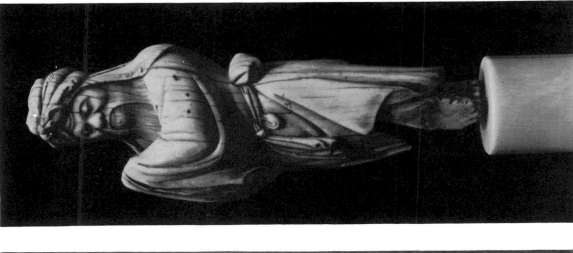

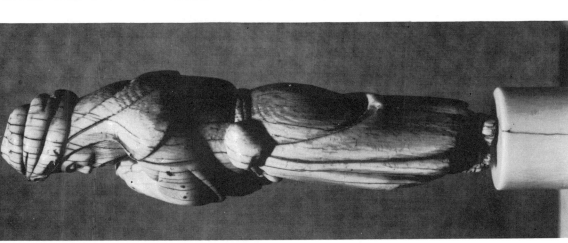

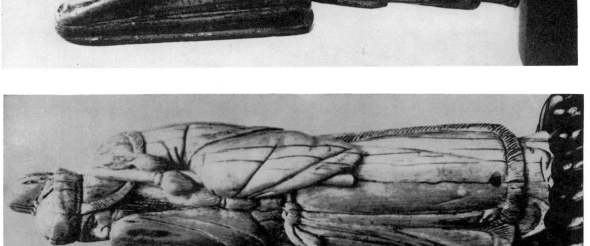

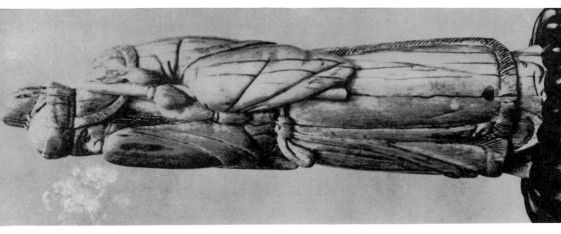

MOURNER OF WESTERN CHINA. (Left).—This wonderful figure, dressed in fur-lined garments most convincingly rendered, holds his hand up to his mouth as though suppressing sobs. Ht. 4¾". Lion Col. Paris.

SUPPLICANT IN CARVED IVORY. (Right).—What could be more moving than this simple carving of an old man lifting his hands in supplication? Ht. 5¾". Lion Collection, Paris.

MING CARVING OF A SUPPLICANT OF CHINESE TUR-KESTAN.—This exceedingly rare figure with its distinctive turban undoubtedly represents some personage of western China or more likely Turkestan. The profile shows the conventional treatment of the back in all details except the wide drape from the turban which covers the shoulders. Ht. c.7". Ralph M. Chait Col. Warren E. Cox.

PLATE 17

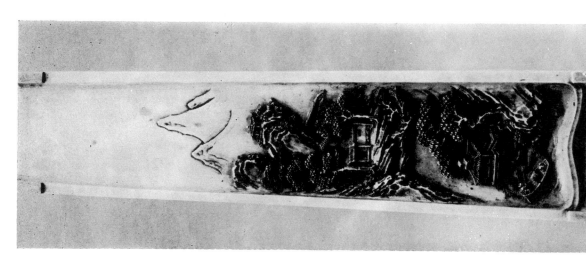

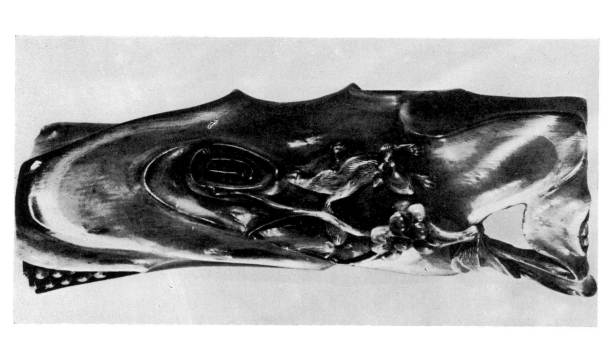

WRIST REST. (Left)—This wrist rest for the scholar's table is typical of the rather bold design in favor during the Ming Dynasty. This piece is stained a deep brown color which brings out the grain. Length 6¼". C. T. Loo & Co., Warren E. Cox Galleries.

WRIST REST. (Right)—Incorrectly called a "brush-holder" is this beautiful wrist rest which is smooth and rounded on the top and carved with a massively conceived landscape design underneath and inside. Ch'ien Lung. L. 8⅞". Metropolitan Museum.

FOSSIL WALRUS TUSK SNUFF BOTTLE. (Above)—The carver of this bottle from fossil walrus tusk relied upon simple, sturdy form and a plain surface to bring out the grain of the material. Ht. 2½". Metropolitan Museum of Art.

VERMILLION PASTE BOX. (Below)—Of the K'ang Hsi period or slightly earlier we show this typical vermillion-box designed to hold the paste with which chop-marks are made with seals. (1662-1722 A.D.) Dia. 3". C. T. Loo & Co. Warren E. Cox Galleries.

PLATE 18

VI. Ch'ing to Modern Ivories

(c. 1644 to 1935)

AS was traced in the last chapter, the great herds of elephants kept by the earlier emperors for ceremonial purposes and possibly use in war, slowly came to be used for mere show and finally dwindled in number to a mere 60 in the time of Ch'ien Lung (1736-1796) and to none by 1901. Only a little mammoth ivory was imported but a great deal of walrus ivory was brought in from the north and of course the trade, which was started in Sung times, in African ivory had continued and grown. Thus while many small objects are of walrus ivory, most very large objects are carved from the great tusks of the African elephant. Such huge examples as the great vase shown in our exhibition of the Frank Lewis Hough collection could only come from such ivory. (Pl. 19) This tremendous piece measures 27¾ inches high and 6½ inches in diameter and is not curved to the shape of a tusk but is straight so that the original diameter of the tusk must have been perhaps 8 to 10 inches. Moreover it had to come from the solid tip of the tusk so that the tapering would have to be accounted for. This wonderful piece is carved with abundant richness and minute detail about the body showing a palace in the mountains with gateways and winding paths, terrace upon terrace where great curving roofs are partly hidden by the trees, and many people of the court each beautifully detailed and executed with masterful life and movement although they are only about a half inch in height. The base and neck are carved in low relief conventional designs of ju-i borders and symmetrical bands of flowers and bats in a design closely resembling that found on enamelled porcelains of the period. About the shoulder are immortals descending upon clouds and on the top of the cover is a group of three more, the central figure holding a ju-i sceptre, the one to the right holding the peach of immortality and the one to the left a halter attached to a beautiful spotted stag. The whole is tinted with soft famille rose colors. The design would lead me to assert with confidence that this piece is of the Tao Kuan reign (1821-1850).

Two other tremendous and superb pieces in the Hough collection (Pl. 20) are the Kwan-yin with crown showing seated Buddhas, large ear-rings, a jeweled gown and a lotus bud and leaf held in the right hand, (This figure is 29 inches tall and could be said to belong to the last two types described in our last chapter; the full faced rather voluptuous "Asiatic" type and the queenly "Sultana" type.) and the other, a wonderfully graceful figure with top-knot of hair, long oval face and beautiful sweeping raiment, holding a basket of flowers and some lilies. This figure is 30 inches high. Both are beautifully stained with various soft colors. Both are of African elephant ivory and both date about 1850 or a little later. I know of no others equal in beauty, perfection and scale.

Of the K'ang Hsi reign (1662-1722) Laufer shows one figure which seems to fit quite properly just a little later than Ming. It is a Buddhistic monk, bald headed as Buddhist monks are, and bright eyed as he preaches the gospel. Laufer says, "He stands there a worthy disciple of Cakyamuni, humble and modest, sincere and fully conscious of the truth of his convictions." This figure is of white ivory touched only with a little black about the eyes to accent them. It is about 11 inches high.

Large vase of Tao Kuan period beautifully detailed with palace scene and immortals about the shoulder and on the cover. The low relief decoration setting these off is much like that found on enamelled porcelains. (1821-1850) Ht. 27¾". *Mrs. Frank Lewis Hough Col. Warren E. Cox Galleries.*

PLATE 19

QUEENLY TYPE OF KWAN YIN OF GREAT SIZE. *(Left)*—Combining the voluptuous, Asiatic type with the queenly type, this beautiful example of polychromed ivory shows the mastery of Northern Chinese craftsmanship, of the 19th century. Ht. 29″.
SPIRITUAL KWAN YIN OF GREAT SIZE. *(Center)*—This tremendous figure is of the most beautiful ethereal expression and shows the superb artistry of North China even in the 19th century. Ht. 30″. *Mrs. Frank Lewis Hough Col., Warren E. Cox Galleries.*
SOUTH CHINESE KWAN YIN OF CARVED IVORY. *(Right)*—This figure might be representative of the "Sultana" type of Kwan Yin. It is of the 19th century and typical of the over-ornate quality of South Chinese work. Ht. 17⅛″. *Metropolitan Museum*
PLATE 20

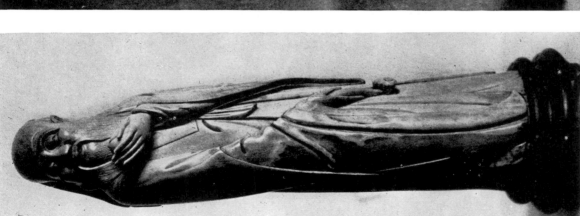

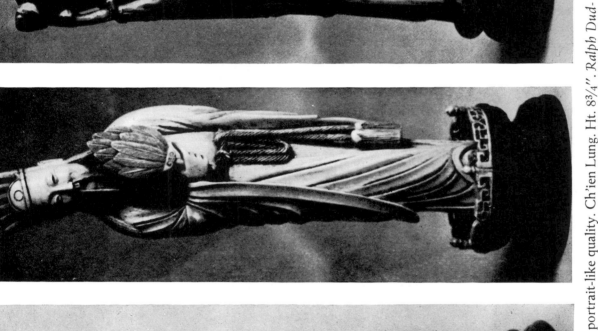

1. A Buddhistic monk in the act of preaching, attributed to the K'ang Hsi reign. Ht. 11″. *Field Museum, Chicago.*

2. THE GOD OF LONGEVITY OR SHOU LAO.— This well represents the K'ang Hsi style. Ht. 9¼″. *Metropolitan Museum.*

3. Although this figure probably represents the Taoist Immortal, Chung-li Ch'uan, it has a very human and portrait-like quality. Ch'ien Lung. Ht. 8¾″. *Ralph Dudley Col.*

4. SHOU LAO THE GOD OF LONGEVITY.—Shou Lao is said to have become indistinguishable from Lao Tsze ("the Old Child"), who is said to have been born with his head white and the countenance of an aged man; the founder of Taoism. He is usually shown with a knotted stick and a scroll or peach. (Ch'ien Lung). Ht. 8″. *Ralph M. Chait Col.*

5. FU HSING, GOD OF HAPPINESS.—The Three Star Gods are representative of Longevity (Shou Hsing or Shou Lao with staff and peach), Rank (Lu Hsing holding a *Ju-i* sceptre) and Happiness. Ch'ien Lung. Ht. 7″. *Ralph M. Chait Col.*

PLATE 21

BUDDHISTIC TRINITY OF CH'IEN LUNG OR EARLIER
PERIOD—Sakyamuni Buddha (or Gautama) in the center with,
to his right, Avalokitésvara (or Kwan Yin) and to his left Maitreya
(or Mi-lei Fo) in polychromed ivory of the Ch'ien Lung, or possibly earlier, period. Ht. 8½". *Mrs. Frank Lewis Hough Col. Warren E. Cox Galleries.*

PLATE 22

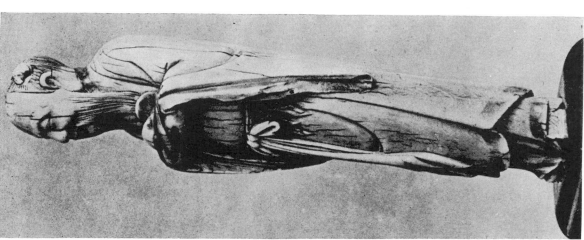

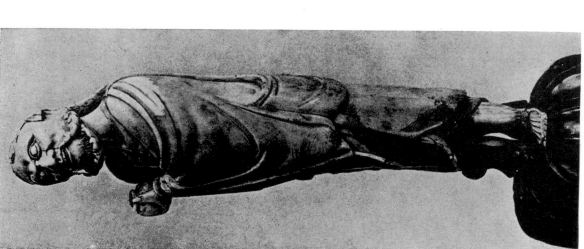

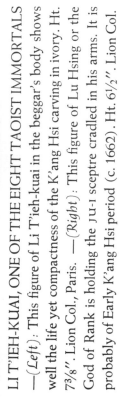

TWO BUDDHISTIC DISCIPLES CALLED LO-HAN OR ARHATS—These two figures of Lo-han or Arhats are shown by Laufer as of the Ch'ien Lung reign. Note the ornate and over detailed quality of the carving. Hts. 10″ and 11″. *Capt. Marshall Field Expedition to China 1923.*

LI T'IEH-KUAI, ONE OF THE EIGHT TAOIST IMMORTALS —*(Left):* This figure of Li T'ieh-kuai in the beggar's body shows well the life yet compactness of the K'ang Hsi carving in ivory. Ht. 7⅜″. Lion Col., Paris. —*(Right):* This figure of Lu Hsing or the God of Rank is holding the JU-I sceptre cradled in his arms. It is probably of Early K'ang Hsi period (c. 1662). Ht. 6½″. Lion Col.

PLATE 23

EIGHTEEN LOHAN IN CARVED IVORY—Note that all of the figures are readily identifiable. However, from the following chart we can recognize at once beginning at the upper left: 1. A-pi-t'eh with his stupa; 3. Kiai-poh-kia with the saint above his shoulder; 6. Tah-mo-to-lo with a tiger, and in the bottom row: 1. Pu-tai-huo-sang with his unmistakable fat belly (Note that he also has a fan which none of our authorities listed); 2. Kia-li-kia with long eye-brows; 5. Na-k'ia-si-na with his alarm-staff; 6. Pan-t'oh-kia with the dragon coming out of his bowl. I am told by Mrs. Antoinette K. Gordon that 7. is Fu-hoa, given by Koji Hoten (p. 195 No. 29) as ringing a bell. The others are more difficult. It will be noted that seven have flywhisks, while our authorities list only four so equipped. Hts. 11". C. T. Loo & Co.

PLATE 24

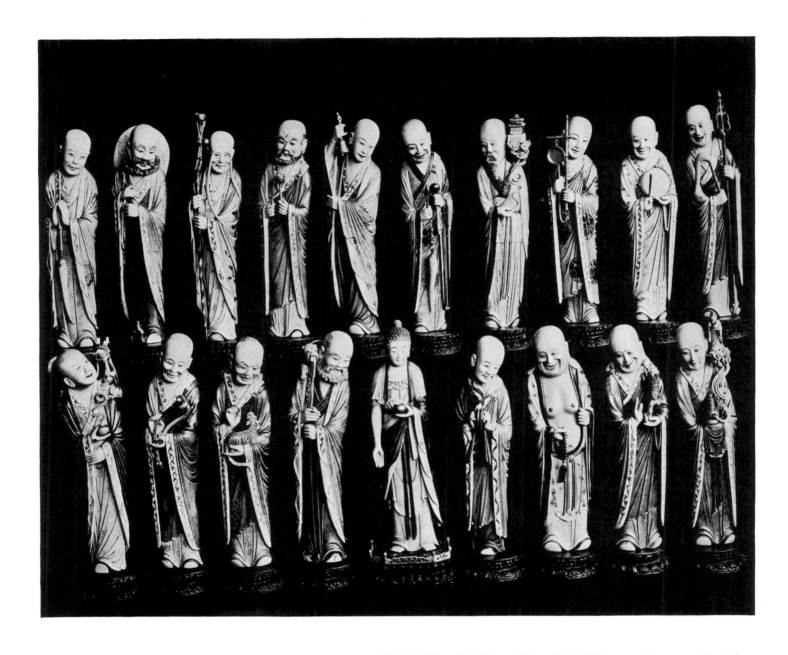

EIGHTEEN LOHAN AND A BUDDHA—Sakyamuni Buddha stands in the center of the bottom row making the varada mudra with his right hand (seal of charity) and holding an alms bowl (patra) in his left hand. Some of the Lohan that can be recognized are: *(Upper left to right)* 1. Possibly No. 13 our list, YIN-KIEH-T'O, with flywhisk. 2. Doubtful. 3. KAI-LI-KIA with long eyebrows, No. 7. 4. Doubtful. 5. KOJI HOTEN gives FU-HOA as ringing a bell. 6. Doubtful. 7. A-PI-T'EH with a stupa, No. 4. 8. Doubtful. 9. Doubtful. 10. NA-K'IA-SI-NA with his alarm-staff (khakkhara), No. 12. 11. PAN-T'OH-KIA with his dragon coming out of the bowl, No. 10. 12. Doubtful. 13. TAH-MO-TO-LO with tiger, No. 18. 14. PA-KU-LAH with mongoose, No. 5. 15. The Buddha. 16. Doubtful. 17. PU-TAI-HUO-SANG with fat belly and rosary, No. 17. 18. Doubtful, possibly POH-T'O-LO because of abhaya mudra. 19. KIAI-POH-KIA with small saint above shoulder. Hts. 9″. *Mrs. Frank Lewis Hough Col. Warren E. Cox Galleries.*

PLATE 25

From Mr. Loo we illustrate a small round box used to contain vermillion for chop-marks. This has a delicate drawing etched into it and into the lines of which black has been rubbed. (Pl. 18)

Of the latter part of the Ming Dynasty, that is, late 16th to early 17th Century, is a group of three figures (Pl. 22) belonging to Mrs. Frank Lewis Hough representing in the center Sâkyamuni Buddha or Gautama, the last earthly incarnation of Buddha, while to his right is Avalokitésvara or Kwan-yin holding the cintâmani, or precious pearl and with left hand in the Vitarka mudrâ with hand at shoulder height, palm outward, fingers extended upward and fore-finger touching the thumb, in the position of the seal of exposition or argument, and, to his left is Maitreya or Mi-lei fo, the future Buddha, the compassionate one, holding in his hand a Kalasa or ch'ing p'ing, pure vessel,'' containing dew or nectar of immortality to sprinkle on the worshippers. In the crowns of the two attendant figures are small figures of Buddha seated on the lotus throne and surrounded with a nimbus of flame or light. The robes are graceful and lovely and the figures stand upon curling lotus blossoms. The expressions are serious and thoughtful conveying an impressive feeling of religious fervor and though this little gem is only 8½ inches tall, it gives an impression of being actually monumental. There are traces of colors most of which are worn off allowing the soft ivory, like flesh, to show through. It is a piece of considerable charm.

In the Ch'ien Lung period (1736-1796) we have from Laufer's book two Buddhist saints or Arhats, called by the Chinese "Lo-han" and actually the celebrated disciples of the Buddha. (Pl. 23) Both have the high foreheads which are characteristic and both have large noses, heavy mustaches and beards. The one stands with his foot on a lion,'' symbolizing the saint's power over the wild animals,'' while in his right hand he holds a branch with the fungus of im-

mortality "ling-chi", really a Taoist emblem, and in his right a fly-brush or "chowry" of yak-tails or coir, an emblem of royalty, the tip of which tickles the lips of the devoted beast. The other figure stands with his foot on the head of a three-legged frog while he conjures a dragon from his alms-bowl. Many of these figures represent mystic beliefs which were sometimes involved and often mixed up by the carvers themselves not unlike the complications in the renderings of some of the European saints. Laufer shows two other sets of two and that is all of the figures of the period he mentions.

Earlier and more likely K'ang Hsi than Ch'ien Lung are the two figures I show from the Lion Collection, Paris. (Pl. 23) The first is a similar lohan (See list following in this chapter) with alms-bowl and the second is the Immortal, Han-Siang-Tseu. A comparison of these figures will show that, as in all things, the Ch'ien Lung ivory carving became more ornate, less inspired and less alive, although it still maintained considerable decorative charm.

A most remarkable set of the Eighteen Lohan we exhibit and illustrate from Mr. C. T. Loo. (Pl. 24) These are large and beautifully carved with wonderfully developed expression; each piece is a real personality. The images of these disciples of Buddha are placed in attendance upon those of Buddha in Chinese temples.

There were only sixteen Lohan, also called Arhat or Arhan, in the pantheon of Indian Buddhism. The literal translation of the word is "fit' or "worthy." In Tibet they are called Sthavira. According to Alice Getty ("Gods of Northern Buddhism," p. 156), "An Arhat is one who has reached the end of the Eight-Fold Path, and is not only perfect himself, but can give perfection to others. Gautama Buddha, before making the Great Vow of the Bodhisattva, was, in one of his incarnations, the Arhat Sumedha." She gives four "Great Bhikshu" to whom Buddha entrusted the propagation of the faith after his death:

75

—1.—*Mahakasyapa*, or as he is more commonly called, *Kâsyapa*, or in Chinese, *Mo Ho Chia Yeh*, the very old but strong and virile disciple, 2.—*Pindola*, or *Manla*, about whom more later, 3.—*Kuntés-pan-t'an*, who was not an Arhat, and 4.—*Rahula*, (See No. 11 in chart following) again about which I shall have more to say in the following chart :—As the names and somewhat involved attri- butes of the Eighteen Lohan are complicated I think the following chart may help to fix them in mind. I have based this chart on that given in the "Hand- book of Chinese Buddhism, by E. J. Eitel, adding to it facts given by C. A. S. Williams in his "Outlines of Chinese Symbolism,' by Alice Getty, Oswald Sirén and others :—

Chart of Eighteen Lohan or Arhats

1. *Pin-tu-lo Po-lo-to-shê, Pindola the Bharadvaja, Pin-t'ou*, or *Manla* (Getty) "the Supreme Phy- sician," *Pu-tung* (the unmoved)

ATTRIBUTES: His head is covered with a hood, his hands with mittens, and he has many bibs about his neck so that his face is scarcely visible. (Getty)

Gaunt and old, he sits with an open book upon his knee and has a mendicant's staff. (Williams)

Thin and ribbed, a book in one hand and alms bowl in the other, sometimes a book held reverently in both hands, sometimes a book on one knee and a mendicant's staff at his side. "When King Asoka summoned his great assembly, Pindola was an old man with white hair and very long eyebrows which he had to hold back in order to see." (Eitel)

STORIES ABOUT HIM: Miss Getty says he is often placed outside of the temple in Japan and, I believe, also in Korea for he remarked the beauty of a woman and so was expelled from the Sixteen. She says that as a Buddha he has the urna, ushnisha, short curly hair, monastic robe and the "meditation mudra" (The Dhyâna mudrâ, with hands lying in the lap, fingers extended and one hand upon the other, palms upward) sometimes having a branch with fruit, or the fruit alone of the Myrobalaus, which looks like a lemon but is five lobed, and he wears a crown of five leaves. It is unusual, she says for a future Budhisattva to have been an Arhat. (Gods of Northern Buddhism p. 43)

Eitel says that Pindola had a retinue of 1000 other arhats, that he was a defender of orthodoxy and had a voice like the roar of a lion. He tells that he could not resist showing off his magical powers and one day he rose in the air, took a sandal-wood bowl off a very high pole and floated about with it over the heads of the crowd. The Master rebuked him for this and sandal-wood was prohibited for making bowls. It was said that at this time he was told not to "take Nirvana" but to remain in existence and protect Buddha's system until the coming of Maitreya.

This is a good example of the difficulties some- times confronting a person who wants to identify some particular figure. Only by comparisons and the process of elimination can success be achieved.

2. *Ka-no-ka Fa-tso, Kanaka the Vatsa*

ATTRIBUTES: None given

STORIES CONCERNING HIM: Williams and Eitel tell us that he had a retinue of 500 other arhats, was a disciple of Buddha and understood all systems both good and bad.

76

3. *Ka-no-ka Po-li-tou-shê, Kanaka the Bharadvaja* Had 900 followers

ATTRIBUTES: Eitel says he was a very hairy old man and sometimes has a small disciple at his side. Also had 600 arhats under him.

Williams also calls him hairy but says he is the "Second Pindola" and calls him Pin-t'ou-lu O-lo-sui-shih, while Eitel puts this "Second Pindola" as one of the two added to the original 16 to make the 18 Arhats at a later time.

4. *Su-p'in-t'e,* or *Subhinda* Had 800 followers

Eitel says the name does not occur in some lists but is found in temples in China, Korea and Japan. When it is not present its place is taken by:—

Nan-t'i-mi-to-lo Ch'ing-yu, or *Nandimitra*

He had 900 followers

ATTRIBUTES: He is a venerable sage with a scroll in his right hand, or simply sitting in an attitude of meditation, or with an alms-bowl and incense-vase beside him, while he holds a sacred book in his left hand, and snaps his fingers of his right hand to show the rapidity with which he attained spiritual insight.

5. *No-kü-lo,* or *Nakula,* also at times *Pa-ku-la, P'u-kü-lo, Pa-no-ka,* or *Vakula,* sometimes called *Kundo-vahan* "Mongoose Bearer." He had 800 followers

ATTRIBUTES: He is shown, according to Getty, like Jambala, with a mongoose under his arm. Eitel says he sometimes has a three-legged-frog under his left arm and sometimes is teaching a little boy at his side. Williams says he teaches the little boy and holds a rosary of 108 beads.

STORIES ABOUT HIM: He was said never to have preached a word (Hard to understand when the figures show him at it!), to have been one of Buddha's great disciples, and there is a story that when King Asoka visited his tope and showed his contempt by offering a penny, Vakula topped him by seriously refusing it.

6. *Po-t'ê-lo,* or *Tan-mo-lo Po-t'o, Tamra Bhadra,* or *Bhadra* Had a retinue of 900 arhats

ATTRIBUTES: He is usually in an attitude of worship with prayer beads or rosary (Williams), also he is shown accompanied by a tiger which he soothes. (Eitel)

STORIES ABOUT HIM: It is said that he was a cousin of Buddha's and one of the great disciples. He was also considered a good teacher.

7. *Ka-li-ka, Kalik* or *Kala,* the *Lion King Kala.* Had 1000 arhats in his retinue.

ATTRIBUTES: He usually is studying a scroll or holding a leaf of a tree. His eye-brows are so long that he has to hold them up from the ground.

8. *Fa-shê-lo-fuh-to-lo, Fa-shê-na-fu-to, Vajraputra* or *Vajriputra* Had 1100 arhats

ATTRIBUTES: He is very hairy, lean and ribbed

9. *Shu-po-ka, Chieh-po-ka, Gobaka, Supaka?, Ka-paka* or *Kuo-pa-ka*

Had 900 followers

ATTRIBUTES: He is shown with a small figure of a saint above his right shoulder or close to his side, sometimes holds a book, or at times sits in contemplation while holding a fan.

10. *Pan-t'o-ka, Panthaka, Pantha,* sometimes called *Maha-Panthaka* (Great Panthaka) to distinguish him from his younger brother Chota Panthaka (Little Panthaka), also called Hsiao-lu (Little Road), while the elder brother was called Ta-lu (Great Road).

(We list the younger brother as No. 16.)

Panthaka the elder had some 1300 followers

ATTRIBUTES: He is shown sitting under a tree, preaching from an open book or holding a scroll. Sometimes he simply sits in profound meditation and at times he charms a "dragon into his bowl." (Eitel) (Note:—this seems different from the Laufer description in which he is conjuring a dragon *out of* the bowl.) Williams says he is at times sitting on a rock reading from a scroll.

STORIES: He was among the first of the great disciples by means of his thought always aimed at excellence. He solved all doubts, and had extraordinary magical powers being able to pass through solids and to reduce himself in size until nothing remained.

11. *Lo-hu-lo*, or *Rahula*

Had 1100 followers

ATTRIBUTES: He has a large "umbrella shaped" head, prominent eyes and a hooked nose. Williams adds that he had bushy eyebrows.

STORIES: He was the son of Buddha and is to die and return as Buddha's son many times.

12. *Na-ka-si-na*, *Nagasena*, or *Seni?*

Had 1200 arhats following him

ATTRIBUTES: He can only be distinguished by his commanding presence.

STORIES: He was a Bhikshu 30 years before attaining Arhatship. He was known as an orthodox expounder and had a ready wit.

13. *Yin-kie-t'ê*, *Yin-chieh-t'o*, *Angida*, *Angaja*, or *Angila*, also *Mu-kie-t'ê*

He had 1300 arhat followers

ATTRIBUTES: In T'ang tradition and later he was shown as a lean old monk with a book containing Indian writing and a staff. Later he was shown as a fat, jolly creature supposed to be Maitreya or his incarnation.

He was perfect in all things and was noted for the cleanliness and fragrance of his body.

14. *Fa-na-p'o-ssu*, or *Vanavasa*

Had 1400 followers

ATTRIBUTES: He sits in a cave meditating with eyes closed. His hands often make a mudra or he nurses his right knee.

15. *A-shih-to*, or *Asita*, or *Ajita?* — but this is doubtful according to Eitel for Ajita is Maitreya the Budhisattva who remains in Tushita Para-

dise and he could not properly be a guardian of Sakyamuni's system.

He had 1500 followers

ATTRIBUTES: An old man with long eyebrows seated nursing his right knee.

It should be noted here that Williams gives *Ajita* as No. 17 on his list despite the above remark by Eitel, he gives the Chinese name as *A-tzu-ta*. I do not know of any other authorities who agree.

16. *Chu-ch'a (t'a) Pan-t'o-ka*, *Chota-Panthaka* (*Little Panthaka*),—or *Pantha* (Williams)— Also *Hsiao-lu* (*Little Road*) (See No. 10. for older brother) 1600 followers

ATTRIBUTES: He appears as an old man under a dead tree which he leans against. He holds a fan in one hand and has the other in the teaching mudrâ (Vitarka mudrâ, hand raised to the height of the shoulder with fingers extended upward except the first which touches the thumb.) Eitel also says he is shown as a venerable sage on a mat-covered seat holding a long staff surmounted with an hare's head.

STORIES: He was at first very dull and stupid, and was scorned by all the other followers of Buddha. On one occasion the King invited Buddha and his disciples to breakfast but Little Pantha was omitted. Buddha refused to sit down until the despised disciple was sent for. He could not remember even one stanza, so Buddha had him repeat, "Sweeping broom," through which he learned that all evil was to be swept away. He could fly through the air and assume any form. One time he produced 500 strange oxen and rode on one.

17. We now come to differences. Eitel says that *Nandimitra* or also *Liang Wu Ti*, Imperial patron of Buddhism who lived about 502 to 550 A.D. might be No. 17. Some Sung temples have Maitreya or rather his supposed incarnation *Pu-tai Ho-shang*, the "calico-bag cushion" monk, who is said to have lived about 6th cen-

tury A.D. but was not honored as a Lohan until modern times. He is, of course fat, and is the patron saint of tobacco-sellers. Williams gives *A-tzu-ta* or *Ajita*, as an old man with a bamboo staff. *Dharmatrata* was added in Sung times and appears as an old man with long hair, who carries a vase and a fly-whisk (chauri) in his hands and has a bundle of books on his back. I do not know where Alan Priest (p. 27 Chinese Sculpture in the Metropolitan Museum of Art) gets his authority for saying that both were added in Sung times for most authorities agree with Eitel that *Pu-tai-ho-shang* is a fairly modern conception.

18. *Pindola the Second*, according to Eitel, and *Po-lo-t'o-she*, another form of *Pindola the Bharadvaja* (No. 1) according to Williams, is the 18th Lohan. He rides a tiger.

Williams also gives *Fa-Chiu*, the Buddhist *Dharmatara*, the "*Great Ukasaka*" and says he is receiving or introducing the 16 (or 18) Lohan.

After considerable research when one commences to identify each of the Lohan in any given group, such as the several from the Mrs. Frank Lewis Hough Collection and from C. T. Loo & Co. which I have exhibited and which are herewith illustrated, it is found to be difficult, nay almost impossible to name each. Having met this condition and fearing that the sensible reader might well question both the authorities and the ability of the writer, I carried my problem to my kind friend Antoinette K. Gordon, the author of "Tibetan Lamaism" a most sound and brilliantly constructed book in which on page 104

she gives the following list as the Tibetan conception. She too spent some time in research and in this freely translated passage from Koji Hoten (p. 196) sums up the situation clearly :—"Theoretically, each 'ra-kan' (the Japanese name for the Arhats or Lohan) should be shown in the attitude which is proper to him; each, has also a distinctive symbol of his own, or a distinctive sign. Practically, it is often very difficult and even impossible to identify them, especially since the artists are not anxious (careful) to represent such and such a ra-kan in the position and with the attribute which should be his. They have sometimes shown a certain ra-kan with the attributes of another." Added to this condition in China and Japan is the further complication that there were first 16, then 18, then 500 and some list even 1200 from which different selections are sometimes made by the artists. In other words one or two may be dropped from a group of 18 and others added because of local enthusiasms or prejudices. However, most often one sees the Eighteen Lohan which I have listed and now to give all of the assistance possible I append the following list arranged in the same arbitrary order as the above list with, after each name, all of the attributes assigned to it by Mrs. Gordon herself in the Tibetan pantheon, by Roerich, also in the Tibetan field, by Eugen Pander (Das Pantheon des Tschang-tscha Hutuktu) and by Walter E. Clark (Two Lamaist Pantheons). As we are interested in Chinese ivories I am using the Chinese names numbered to correspond with the above list. These are from Pander.

Combined List from Mrs. Antoinette K. Gordon's Lists of the Eighteen Lohan

1. *Pin-tu-lo-poh-lo-to* (Pindola)—holds a pustaka (flat book of palm leaves) and a patra (alms bowl) (Gordon)
   book and bowl (Roerich)
   book and alms bowl (Pander)
   ? (Clark)
   hood, mittens and bibs (See Getty above) is thin, has staff and long eyebrows (above list)

2. *Kia-noh-kia-fah-ts'o* (Kanaka the Vatsa) — holds jeweled pasa (noose) (Gordon)
   lasso (Roerich)
   noose (Pander)
   jeweled noose (Clark)
   no attributes given (above list)

3. *Kia-noh-kia-poh-li-to-ngan* (Kanaka the Bharadvaja)—meditation mudra (dhyana mudra) holds a dhvaja (round banner of victory) (Gordon)
   meditation (Roerich)
   hands folded in lap (Pander)
   meditation (Clark)
   (Second Pindola) hairy (above list)

4. *A-pi-t'eh* (Subhinda)—holds a stupa (Gordon)
   stupa (Roerich)
   stupa (Pander)
   stupa (Clark)
   none of these give *Su-p'in-t'e* whom Eitel gives no attributes for, nor *Nan-t'i-mi-to Ch'ing-yu* scroll, alms bowl and incense vase beside him, or book in left hand while he snaps fingers of his right hand, though Eitel says they do occur in temples in China.

5. *Pa-ku-lah* (Nakula)—holds a mongoose vomiting jewels (a nakula) (Gordon)
   rat vomiting jewels (Roerich)
   mongoose vomiting jewels (Pander)
   mongoose vomiting jewels (Clark)
   mongoose, three-legged frog, little boy or rosary of beads (above list)

6. *Poh-t'o-lo* (Tamra Bhadra) — holds a pustaka (flat book of palm leaves), is in dhyana mudra (meditation mudra); his right hand may be in vitarka mudra (that of exposition or argument) (Gordon)
   book, or meditation (Roerich)
   book in left hand (Pander)
   abhaya mudra (the seal of assurance or fearlessness—the hand raised to the height of the shoulder, palm outward and fingers upward) or dhyana mudra (see above) (Clark)
   worship with beads (above list)

7. *Kia-li-kia* (Kalik or Kala) — holds two golden trinkets (Gordon)
   two golden trinkets (Roerich)
   golden ear-rings (Pander)
   two trinkets ? (Clark)
   long eyebrows (above list) holds a leaf, studies scroll

8. *Fah-ngan-lo-fuh-to* (Vajraputra)—holds a fan or camara (fly-whisk); his right hand in vitarka mudra (hand the same as in abhaya mudra (see No. 6) with first, second or third finger touching tip of thumb) (the mudra of exposition or argument) (Gordon)
   fan in left hand, right hand raised (Roerich)
   flywhisk (Pander)

flywhisk (Clark)

hairy, lean and ribbed (above list)

9. *Kiai-poh-kia* (Kapaka)—holds a pustaka (Flat book of palm leaves) (Gordon)

book (Roerich)

book in both hands (Pander)

book (Clark)

small saint above shoulder or close to side, book or fan (above list)

10. *Pan-t'oh-kia* (Panthaka or Pantha)—holds a pustaka (flat book) (Gordon)

book (Roerich)

preaching from a book (Pander)

book (Clark)

under tree preaching from book, or holds scroll, or dragon in bowl (above list)

11. *Lo-ku-lo* (Rahula)—holds a crown (Gordon)

crown (Roerich)

crown of the Buddha (Pander)

crown (Clark)

large head, large eyes, hooked nose (above list)

12. *Na-k'ia-si-na* (Nagasena) — holds a kalasa (vase for holding ambrosia) and a khakkhara (alarm staff with large ring holding small rings) (Gordon)

khakkhara (Roerich)

incense burner and alarm staff (Pander)

incense burner and khakkhara (Clark)

commanding presence (above list)

13. *Yin-kieh-t'o* (Angida)—holds a fan and incense burner (Gordon)

fan and incense burner (Roerich)

incense burner and flywhisk (Pander)

flywhisk and incense burner (Clark)

lean with book of Indian writing, staff,—later is fat as Maitreya incarnation.

14. *Fah-na-p'o-si* (Vanavasa) — holds a fan or camara (flywhisk); his left hand in tarjani mudra (the menacing mudra, fingers doubled into a fist, except index finger, which is raised in menacing attitude) (Gordon)

fan (Roerich)

flywhisk (Pander)

flywhisk on long stick (Clark)

in cave with eyes closed, nurses right knee, or hands in a mudra (above list)

15. *A-si-to* (Asita or Ajita) — is in meditation mudra (dhyana mudra; hands lying in lap, fingers extended and palms up), his head is covered (Gordon)

meditation, head covered (Roerich)

mudra (Pander)

head covered, hands in meditation (Clark)

old, long eyebrows, nurses right knee (above list)

16. *Cu-t'u-pan-t'oh-kia* (Little Panthaka or Pantha)—is meditating (Gordon)

meditating (Roerich)

? (Pander)

meditation (Clark)

leans on a dead tree, is old, vitarka mudra, may sit on mat-covered seat and hold long staff with hare's head at top (above list)

Two religious supporters added later:

17. *Pu-tai-huo-sang*—fat, happy, often surrounded by children, wears a shawl about his shoulders which leaves his belly bare. (Gordon)

sack and rosary (Pander)

rosary and jewel (Clark)

fat (above list)

18. *Tah-mo-to-lo* — (Dharmatala) has long hair and carries fan and vase from which rises incense in which is an image of Amitabha; he has a tiger at his side and sometimes holds an umbrella; his robe is elaborate and his hair is often done up into a high chignon on top of his head; he often also carries a frame on his back containing books. (Gordon)

A RARE GROUP OF THE EIGHTEEN LOHAN IN SEATED POSITIONS—It is not necessary to list the ones of these which are readily identified, but we might add that the figure fourth from the upper left is KIA-LI-KIA (No. 7 our list) shown with his golden trinkets and this would make the last one to the right in the center row probably A-SI-TO (15), the other listed with long eyebrows. Hts. 5½". *Mrs. Frank Lewis Hough Col. Warren E. Cox Galleries.*

PLATE 26

THE EIGHT TAOIST IMMORTALS or "PA HSIEN".—It is rare
to find these immortals done in seated positions. They are left to
right: Lu Tung-pin with sword and flywhisk, Han Hsiang-ku with
basket of flowers, Ho Hsien-ku (the woman with lotus), Lan T'sai-
ho with flute, Chung-li Ch'uan with fan, Chang Kuo-lao with bamboo tube, Ts'ao Kuo-chiu with hu (court tablet) and finally Li
T'ieh-kuai in the beggar's body. Hts. 5½". *Mrs. Frank Lewis
Hough Col. Warren E. Cox Galleries.*

PLATE 27

THE EIGHT TAOIST IMMORTALS or "PA HSIEN".—These legendary beings, described in the text, are: *(Left to right)* 1. Li T'ieh-kuai with his crutch and the beggar's body. 2. Chang Kuo-lao holding a bamboo tube containing two sticks, from which he brings his paper mule. 3. Chung-li Ch'uan with his fan. 4. Han Hsiang-tzu with a flower basket. 5. Ho Hsien-ku, the only female, who carries a lotus flower. 6. Lan T'sai-ho has a flute. 7. Lu Tung-pin with his sword the handle of which sticks up behind his left shoulder. 8. Ts'ao Kuo-chiu who holds a ceremonial court tablet. Hts. 9".
Mrs. Frank Lewis Hough Col. Warren E. Cox Galleries.

PLATE 28

books, incense burner, flywhisk Image of Amitabha (Pander)

incense burner, staff (Clark)

long hair, vase, flywhisk and bundle of books on back. (above list)

It is hoped that the above chart will help to identify most groups of the Eighteen Lohan and we are highly indebted to Mrs. Gordon for her invaluable help in detailed notes, and particularly for the clarification of the general situation.

From the collection of Mrs. Frank Lewis Hough, I am able to illustrate two superb groups of the eighteen Lohan (Pl. 26 & 27), one unusual one with the figures all seated, and one beautifully conceived in richly colored raiment. This latter is exhibited surrounding a central figure in the bottom row of Sakyamuni Buddha making the varada mudra with his right hand (seal of charity) and holding a patra (alms bowl) in his left hand. The expressions of these are alive and beautifully conceived.

Other groups in the Hough collection represent the Eight Taoist Immortals or the "Pa Hsien" as they are called (Pl. 28). These are purely legendary and each figure carries some special object related to his story. Thus left to right in the illustration we have:

1. *Li T'ieh-kuai* about whom it was told that his spirit could leave his body at will and journey great distances. Once when he was doing this a tiger found his spiritless body lying on the ground and ate it so that when the spirit returned there was no body for it. Thus Li T'ieh-kuai had to enter the body of a beggar who had just died, and he has remained in that body ever since.

2. *Chang Kuo-lao* is said to have a paper mule in the bamboo tube he holds and this is changed by him at will into a real animal on which he is capable of travelling incredible distances. When he comes to his destination the animal is changed back into pa-

per, rolled up and put into the tube again. Thus he is shown either riding a mule or holding the bamboo tube.

3. *Chung-li Ch'uan* is always shown holding a fan with which he is capable of brushing away all evil.

4. *Han Hsiang-tzu* holds a flower-basket in one hand and the fungus of immortality in the other.

5. *Ho Hsien-ku* is the only female in the group and she holds a lotus blossom and leaf, a symbol of fertility and also of the transcendental beauty which rises above the mud. This symbol is also given Kwan Yin at times.

6. *Lan T'sai-ho* has a flute with which he can soothe the soul and quiet savage beasts.

7. *Lu Tung-pin* carries a sword on his back with the handle sticking up over his shoulder just as a present-day Balinese carries his kris.

8. *Ts'ao Kuo-chiu* holds a ceremonial court tablet or "hu" such as we have described above.

In the Hough collection there are three sets of these figures standing in richly colored costumes while the fourth shows the beings seated.

Other groups show a sort of personification of the twelve flowers representing each month of the year (Pl. 30). These are not legendary figures and the artist had to use more of his own imagination to create the various personalities. A group of four seated figures represent the "Four Vocations": fishing, learning, woodcutting and husbandry. Another group shows four ladies playing the well-known Chinese musical instruments: 1.—the Shêng or reed organ, 2.—the Hsiao or ceremonial flute, 3.—the San hsien or three stringed guitar, and 4.—the P'ai hsiao or pandean pipes, as they are shown left to right. There are various types of instruments and these are four of the commonest. The figures show a pensive sort of concentration. While still another beautiful group of fourteen including two children and twelve slender girls are playing various instru-

LARGE IVORY FIGURE. *(Left)*—This large figure is probably of Ho Hsien-ku, the female Taoist Immortal and she has a type of voluptuous beauty which is appealing to western as well as eastern eyes. Ht. 22½″. C. T. Loo & Co. Warren E. Cox Galleries. LIFE-LIKE PORTRAIT IN IVORY *(Right)*—Undoubtedly a portrait showing wonderful personality, humor and intelligence. Note the broad, plastic lines and fine movement. Ht. 23¼″. Ch'ien Lung period (1736-1796 A.D.) C. T. Loo & Co. Warren E. Cox Galleries.

PLATE 29

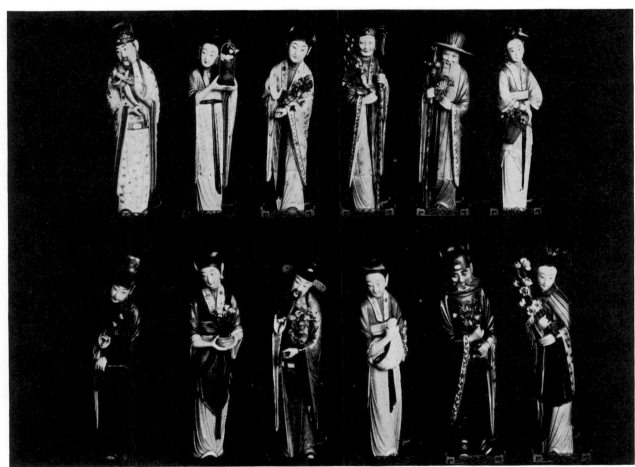

MUSICIANS AND DANCERS OF THE COURT. (Above)—
A set of court dancers and musicians having lovely, slender gowns
and seeming to move rhythmically. Hts. 6½". Mrs. Frank Lewis
Hough Col. Warren E. Cox Galleries. FLOWER MONTHS.
(Below)—A set of twelve carved ivory figures representing the
flowers of each month of the year. Hts. 9". Mrs. Frank Lewis
Hough Col. Warren E. Cox Galleries.

PLATE 30

FIGURES OF LEGEND AND HISTORY. *(Top)*—Behind every
one of these figures there is a story to be told, a meaning to unfold;
some heroic deed of the distant past or some iniquity that histori-
ans felt should be remembered. Hts. 4¼″ to 10½″. *Mrs. Frank
Lewis Hough Col., Warren E. Cox Galleries.*
GROUPS WITH CHILDREN. *(Bottom)*—These groups show
ancient sages and men of importance with children. Hts. c. 5½″.
Mrs. Frank Lewis Hough Col., Warren E. Cox Galleries.

PLATE 31

FOUR MUSICIANS.—Four lovely ladies, probably of the court, playing Chinese musical instruments: 1. Shêng (reed organ), 2. Hsiao (ceremonial flute), 3. San hsien (three stringed guitar), 4. P'ai hsiao (pandean pipes).

THE FOUR VOCATIONS.—Fishing, learning, woodcutting and husbandry. It seems that the scholar has just read a *risqué* story at which the others are laughing. Hts. 6¼". *Mrs. Frank Lewis Hough Col., Warren E. Cox Galleries.*

PLATE 32

ments and dancing with an incense-burner, a sword, a basket of flowers, beads etc. The costumes seem to impart perfectly the graceful, swirling movement to these lovely figures.

Having no especial legendary character but significant of the life of the country are the small groups showing parents with adored children, a girl with a peony, an old man leaning against a dead tree and such genre subjects. Truly the ivory carver presents to us all that is part of the idealized life of the people! And, in a sense, the real and the traditional are one. Thus an old man is shown as a teacher with a little boy at his knee and he becomes a symbol for all teachers, while a figure of Kwan Yin holding a child in her arms, which in turn holds a lotus blossom on which has lighted a large fly, much to the amusement of both, is so human that it seems rather a portrait of some real person than the idealized conception of a goddess; and the figure of *Lu Sing* (the deer god or god of long life) is a very human and even humorous old man.

One of the rarest of the groups is that showing the Emperor or a high official watching a quail-fight (Pl. 36). He is seated before a teak table in which is sunk a large ivory dish holding two quail which are battling to the death. Each bird is attended by an eunuch standing either side of the table and behind them with cage and bird in hand stand two keepers or possibly owners. Quail fighting was a favorite sport in the old days and birds were bred for their abilities much as the western world bred fighting-cocks.

Many historical personages are shown by our ivory carvers. Thus one set of three figures shows in the center Kuan Kung, Kuan Ti or Kuan Yü who lived in the north in Shansi province in the days following the breaking up of the Han Dynasty (Pl. 37). He was a native of Kiai Chow and rose into celebrity toward the end of the 2nd century in the

struggles which ushered in the Three Kingdoms. Originally he was simply a seller of bean curd until 184 A.D. when he met Liu Pei at the time he was going to take up arms in defense of the house of Han. He was made a baron by the regent Ts'ao Ts'ao and remained loyal to his adopted leader and to Chang Fei all his life through many vicissitudes. He was finally beheaded by Sun K'üan. Later he was canonized by Hwei Tsung early in the 12th century and finally raised in 1594 by Ming Wan Li to the rank of God of War.

On the left is Liu Pei, a distant kinsman of the imperial house of Han who rose from the humble occupation of selling straw shoes to lead a body of volunteers against the Yellow Turban Rebellion in 185 A.D. Establishing himself in Sze-ch'wan province he fought against Ts'ao Ts'ao and the house of Wu and became one emperor of the Three Kingdoms. On the right is Chang Fei a butcher and wine-seller who became bosom friend of Kuan Yü and Liu Pei and fought with them until he was assassinated by Fan Kiang.

Another historical personage is Hsiang Fei, who was the beautiful wife of the Muhammedan Prince of Zungaria, Eastern Mongolia. (Pl. 38) Her husband was killed in the war with Ch'ien Lung and she was brought to court to become a concubine of the Emperor. She refused and in the end took her life rather than give in to the amorous advances of the Manchu Emperor who mourned her and conferred the posthumous title of Senior Concubine upon her. Her virtue and loyalty have always appealed to the Chinese mind and though an alien she is included among the Five Famous Beauties of China. The Hough collection includes two beautiful renderings of her.

Another great beauty was Wang Chao-chun who was sent from the court of the Han Emperor Yuan Ti (48-33 B.C.) to be the bride of the Hunnish

FAMILY GROUPS. *(Top)*—Five family groups of old men and women with little boys, playing with a ram, sacred deer, birds and flowers. Hts. 5" to 6½". *Mrs. Frank Lewis Hough Col., Warren E. Cox Galleries.*

(Bottom)—Six small groups of figures, some with children. Hts. 2" to 8¼". *Mrs. Frank Lewis Hough Col., Warren E. Cox Galleries.*

PLATE 33

THE TEACHER.—An old man teacher with a kindly smile as he considers the words of the little boy at his knee. Ht. 10½".

KUAN YIN WITH CHILD.—Figure of Kuan Yin with beads and a child which holds the stem of a lotus-blossom on which is an amusing fly, over which they are both smiling. Ht. 20".

TAOIST IMMORTAL.—LuHsing (God of Long Life). This immortal in the form of an old man holds a sika deer, the sacred deer of China, on some banana leaves and offers it the fungus of immortality. Ht. 12". All photos, *Mrs. Frank Lewis Hough Col , Warren E. Cox Galleries.*

PLATE 34

FIVE MUSICIANS.—The top three are holding (*Left to right*):
1. p'ai hsiao (pandean pipes), 2. p'i pa (balloon guitar), 3. san
hsien (three stringed guitar). The bottom two hold: 1. shêng (reed
organ), 2. hsiao (ceremonial flute). Hts. 8½". *Ralph M. Chait
Col., Warren E. Cox Galleries.*

PLATE 35

QUAIL FIGHT.—This group shows an Emperor or high official watching a quail fight in a large bowl tended by two eunuchs and the keepers of the birds. This was an ancient sport in China. Ht. c. 10". *Mrs. Frank Lewis Hough Col., Warren E. Cox Galleries.*

PLATE 36

THREE HEROES—In the center is Kuan Ti, Kuan Yü or Kuan Kung, a hero of A.D. 219 who was later, in Ming times, made God of War and one of the Gods of Literature. Ht. 5½". To his right is Liu Pei who became the first emperor of the Minor Han Dynasty in 221 A.D. Ht. 6¾". To his left is Chang Fei a noted warrior who later became one of the gods specially worshipped by butchers. He is reputed to have pursued the trade of butcher and wine seller, from which he emerged in A.D. 184, to join the above heroes. Ht. 8".
PLATE 37

A GREAT BEAUTY OF CHINA—One of two carvings in the Hough Col. of Hsiang Fei, the wife of the Mohammedan Prince of Zungaria, Eastern Mongolia, who was brought to Peking to become the concubine of Emperor Ch'ien Lung, after her husband had been killed in the wars. She refused the Manchu Emperor and took her life rather than give in to him. The Chinese include her among the Five Famous Beauties although she was of alien blood. Ht. 10". *Mrs. Frank Lewis Hough Col. Warren E. Cox Galleries.*
PLATE 38

WANG CHAO-CHUN—The famous beauty Wang Chao-chun was sent from the court of the Han Emperor Yuan Ti (48-39 B.C.) to be the bride of a Hsiung Nu or Hunnish chieftain in Mongolia. Sowerby points out that the carver has given the figures queues which were not worn until China was conquered by the Manchus 16 centuries later. Ht. 6″ and 5⅜″. *Mrs. Frank Lewis Hough Col. Warren E. Cox Galleries.*

PLATE 39

chieftain or Hsiung Nu in Mongolia. (Pl. 39) She is shown travelling with her escort on horse back and conversing with attendants. Sowerby points out that the carver was guilty of an anachronism in that he shows the figures with queues, "which were not worn in China till after the conquest of the Manchus fully 16 centuries later than the event portrayed." He goes on, "This is all the more remarkable in view of the fact that the female figures are shown in the ancient dress and coiffeur." Thus our carvers are not infallible in their conceptions.

Nude figures in Chinese art are rare and to quote Arthur de Carle Sowerby writing in the China Journal in September of 1936, after he had lived there for many years, "Nevertheless nude ivory figures of women are to be found, but for the most part they have been carved for a very special purpose. (Pl. 40) According to the etiquette of the old style practice of medicine in China it was considered highly improper for a physician to see the naked form of a female patient or any part of her body. Also it was considered indelicate on the part of the lady to mention any part of her anatomy to the physician. To overcome the difficulties that such reticence naturally placed in the way of the physicians called in to diagnose and treat sick ladies, the former had the ivory carvers make them small figures of nude women in repose showing in intimate detail every organ. One of these figures would be taken to the bedside of the patient, who would put her hand through the folds of the curtains that hid her from the physician's view and touch the exact spot on the figure that was causing her trouble. The physician would then feel his patient's pulse, ask a few innocuous questions, make his diagnosis and give her a prescription." After this interesting account he goes on to say that, "Some of these little ivory figurines are extremely beautiful, but they are not easy to come by, since native curio dealers display considerable reticence in showing them to customers." The exam-

ple we show in the Hough collection has considerable charm and appears to have fallen asleep while examining a scroll. Note that the bound feet are properly shod in dainty slippers to cover the bound feet.

The Frank Lewis Hough Collection also includes a number of objects of carved and stained ivory such as the beautiful *pi ch'ung* or brush-holder showing some dignitary seated on a balcony surrounded by courtiers and ladies while below him in the palace grounds there are many children at play. This piece is remarkable in its detail and quality of carving as can be seen on comparison with the three shown from the Metropolitan Museum. One of these has an engraved line decoration of charm but showing nowhere nearly the interest and beauty of the scholar's set in the Hough collection in which there are two not only engraved but also treated with red and black lacquer. (Pl. 42) These are reported to have come from the ancestral home of Li Hung Chang in Nanking.

It should be noted that most of these things came from northern Honan province and Hopeh (or Chihli) province, many from about Peiping. They are not modern and have in no sense been carved for the trade with the western world, but were made without doubt for wealthy officials and Manchu Princes. Their freshness testifies that they have been put away these many years.

From the C. T. Loo collection we show a charming wine-set consisting of one pot and two cups bearing the nien hao of Ch'ien Lung in seal form and undoubtedly of that reign. (Pl. 42) The low relief decoration with tao t'ieh or monster-head motive is strong and wonderful in workmanship reminding one of the relief decorations on ancient bronzes and jades. Also two small boxes in the form of quails are superbly executed and so soft looking that one feels inclined to stroke them.

The table screens on plate 43 from the Metropolitan Museum of Art also show fine relief carving and

98

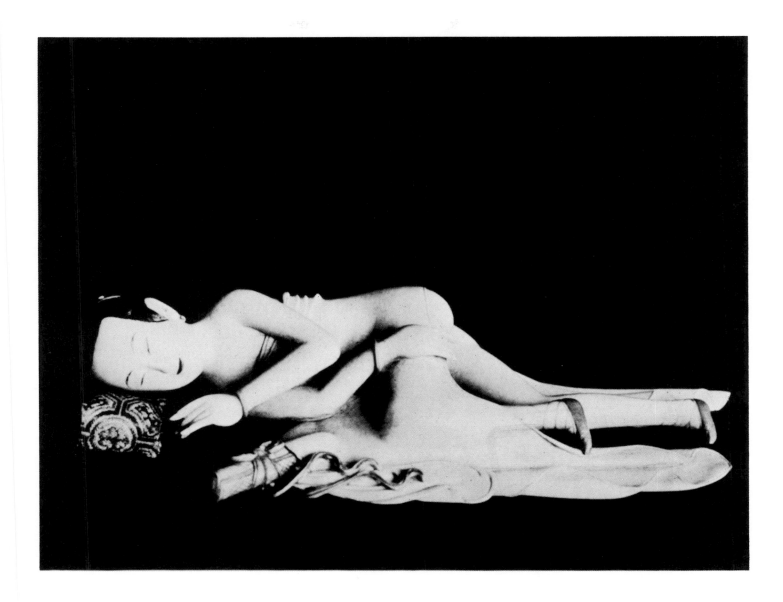

A DOCTOR'S MODEL—This type of partially nude figure was used to indicate to a doctor where a woman might be feeling ill. It was not thought proper for the physician to see the patient. Such figures are rare. Length 7″. *Mrs. Frank Lewis Hough Col. Warren E. Cox Galleries.*

PLATE 40

(Top, left)—A *pi ch'ung* or brush holder of carved ivory showing dignitary surrounded by attendants in a palace, while all about the grounds there are children playing. Ht. 9". *Mrs. Frank Lewis Hough Col., Warren E. Cox Galleries.*

(Top, right)—This brush-holder is made of the natural hollow end of a small tusk or "scrivello" of the type used for billiard balls. Not many of these get to China. Ht. 5¼". Tao Kuan Period.

(Bottom, left)—This typical brush-holder in deeply carved high relief is of Cantonese workmanship and of the 19th or 20th century. Ht. 6⅜". *Metropolitan Museum of Art.*

(Bottom, right)—Brush holder and stand of African ivory of the 20th century. South Chinese carving. Ht. 4". *Metropolitan Museum of Art.*

PLATE 41

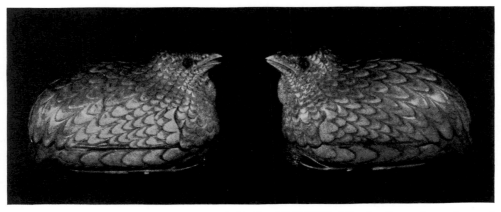

SCHOLAR'S SET. (*Top*)—Ivory furnishings for a desk, consisting of two brush-pots with covers, two screens and one four-fold screen decorated with black lacquer. Panels 4″ by 8″. Brush-pots 10″ high. *Mrs. Frank Lewis Hough Col., Warren E. Cox Galleries*. (*Center*)—This beautiful wine-set bears the nien hao of Ch'ien Lung (1736-1796 A.D.) and is of the period. The design undoubtedly derives from ancient bronze ones. Ht. 4½″. *C. T. Loo & Co., Warren E. Cox Galleries*.

PAIR OF QUAIL BOXES. (*Bottom*)—Two beautiful small boxes in the form of resting quails are of the Ch'ien Lung period (1736-1796 A.D.) and have a warm, pleasant tone. Length 4″. *C. T. Loo & Co., Warren E. Cox Galleries*.

PLATE 42

CH'IEN LUNG SCREEN.—One of a pair, showing the front and back. Note broad areas are left to bring out grain of the material; even details of faces left out. Ht. 10¼".

DESIGN FOR RUG.— Often the Chinese Imperial Household ordered artists in other mediums to make designs for their rug weavers. This example is in relief carved and colored ivory. L. 6⅜". *Metropolitan Museum of Art.*

CH'IEN LUNG SCREEN.— Front and back of one of a pair of Ch'ien Lung (1736-1796) screens in relief carved ivory. Note that the design leaves broad spaces in which the grain of the ivory makes beautiful texture. Ht. 10⅜". *Metropolitan Museum of Art.*
PLATE 43

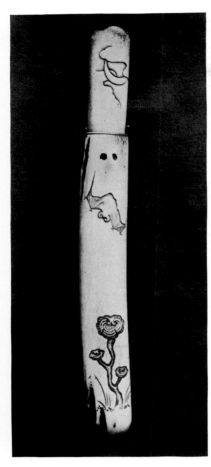
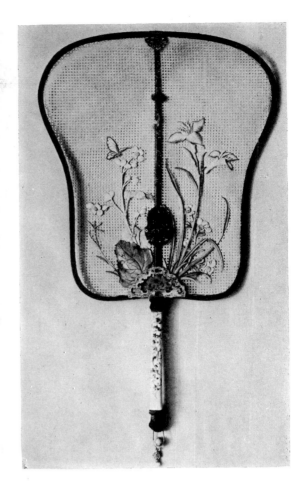

(*Top, left*)—This pendant of pierced ball within pierced ball is typical of the Cantonese work which shows shallow ingenuity rather than any true artistic merit. The piercing is done with drills. The balls are separated one from another with L-shaped knives.

(*Top, center*)—This pipe holder and similar brush holders for the scholars show great refinement of taste. Note the economy of the design of moon-and-clouds, bat for happiness, and fungus of immortality. Ch'ien Lung (1736-1796 A.D.)

(*Top, right*) — This fan is delicately decorated with low relief flowers on a woven ivory ground and is colored, while the handle has lacquer ornamentation. L. 22¼".

(*Left*)—Typical of the South Chinese carving is this fan brisé carved à jour for the European market with lace-like detail. L. 6½".

(*Above*)—This 19th century fan carved in South China has a decoration of the Eight Taoist Immortals. L. 7⅝". All photographs, *Metropolitan Museum of Art*.

PLATE 44

economy of detail, while one of the finest ivory pieces the museum owns is the plaque carved in low relief and colored to show the design for a rug. It was evidently the custom to have artists in various mediums make designs for the rug weavers. I show an interesting Korai porcelain one in "Pottery & Porcelain" figure 416 which has Persian influence. This piece is now in the Boston Museum. Quite possibly these designs in ivory and porcelain were done at imperial command.

In contrast to the North China work, we find that the same commercial influences from Europe that brought about the decadence in porcelain design were at work also among the workers in ivory. To show this I have assembled on plate 44 three fans and a pierced ball pendant from the Metropolitan Museum of Art which have little to recommend them but multiplication of detail and a lace-like delicacy. It

will be noted that the figure finial of the pendant is very poorly carved. These men had become mere craftsmen and were no longer artists. In contrast the reader will find that the pipe holder (Pl. 44) is a wonderful conception. Here a sickle moon cuts through the clouds revealing a bat, symbol of happiness, gayly flitting over a vigorous fungus which is the symbol of immortality. The details are exquisite yet the design is so economical that none of them could be removed without harming it.

I have tried in this small volume to give the reader an idea of the romance and preciousness of the material, ivory, and to show what the Chinese did with it through the past four thousand years or so. Now a word about the working of it and then I hope that some will become collectors. It is too much to hope that any of us people of the western hemisphere might rival them in the art.

VII. The Working of Ivory

THE WORLD has known for centuries that the working of ivory takes patience and highly developed skill. The tools are simple not varying much be they Hindu, Chinese or Japanese. There are saws of both the leaf and band types, thin and fine for the material is valuable and the cut has to be as delicately made as is possible. Some of the leaf saws have rounded ends and some are almost rectangular, being about three times as long as they are wide. Heavy shears, like metal shears, are used to cut thin sheets. Various paring knives and finishing knives have special shapes and in Japan some are named after certain well known carvers. Rasps and files of triangular, rat-tail and flat types are used in various sizes and many various shaped chisels make different shaped grooves or gouges. The drills are primitive and are operated with a drill-bow. There are also small hammers, compasses and finally rabetting plane irons for ornamental work about the bases and the making of beadings. The turning-lathe was not used in early times and its marks, which may appear on the base of a figure or group, are signs of fraud.

In starting the work the first thing that has to be determined is the depth of the hollow part of the tusk. For this purpose a straight steel rod some 18 inches or more in length with a transverse handle is used. Dr. George Frederick Kunz (Ivory and the Elephant p. 244) says, "The measurers have, however, to be on their guard against a trick practised by some dishonest natives or intermediary dealers, who fill up from 2 to 6 inches of the hollow with lead, at once causing the solid part to appear to be longer than it really is, and increasing the weight of the tusk several pounds. The lead costs but a few cents a pound, but the apparent ivory weight is paid for at the rate of two or three dollars or more per pound, and the finest ivory is often at the broadest end of the tusk." Usually the hollow end is employed for certain specific objects such as the brush holders for a scholar's desk. These are seldom, if ever, exactly round, which in a way adds to their charm.

The solid pieces are carefully sawed to proper lengths for the work in hand and the outside enamel knocked off or cut away. Temperatures have to be watched. Dr. Kunz says, "Although extremes of temperature are not so serious for ivory as a sudden draft, still at the docks in London, where the ivory consignments are stored, explosions are occasionally heard as loud as pistol shots, when a sudden change of temperature manifests itself." In this connection we might add that it is best to keep some small dish with water in any case in which ivories are kept so that the air does not get too hot with the artificial illumination employed.

The methods of blocking-out figures is much that employed by any carver. The details are slowly developed and finally the drilling and cutting or filing of the undercuts slowly brings the work to completion. In two things in particular the master shows his skill:—first in the wonderful foresight of the original conception and second in the perfection of detail; though his work may have less fancy detail yet it is wonderfully finished and polished; just the way two grooves in the fold of a piece of material approach each other can disclose the sure hand of a master.

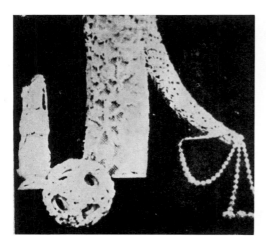

A CANTON IVORY SHOP.—By the dexterous use of a fine drill, this Cantonese carver achieves marvels of workmanship, such as the two shelves of pieces shown. Hollowing out the ivory in intricate designs is Canton's specialty. Careful selection and grading of tusks are most important. Note comparative size (Right). Arthur de Carle Sowerby in the China Journal.

PLATE 45

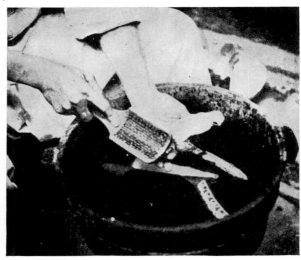

(*Top, left*)—Hippopotamus tusks ready to be carved. (*Top, right*) — Carver's tools. (*Center, left*) — Sawing off the rough ends. (*Center, right*)—Painting on the design. (*Bottom, left*)—Carving out the design. (*Bottom, right*)—Scrubbing the carved ivories. *Arthur de Carle Sowerby.*

PLATE 46

A SHANGHAI IVORY WORKSHOP. (*Top*)—Ivory carving factory in the Native City in Shanghai. (*Center*)—Sawing a tusk in sections. (*Bottom*) — At work upon sections of elephant tusks, carving them into figurines. *Arthur de Carle Sowerby*.

PLATE 47

(*Top*) — Cleaning and polishing the carved ivory pieces. (*Center*) — Putting the final touches, such as tinting and polishing with a soft cloth on the finished carvings. (*Bottom*) A family of ivory carvers. *Arthur de Carle Sowerby*.

PLATE 48

Spurious imitations of antique ivories are common and the cracks are brought into being by dipping the piece into hot water and then baking it in an oven. The staining is done with fumigation of the piece with tobacco, tannin, or moist hay or by immersing it in a solution of ochre, dye or even tea. Dr. Kunz says, "A cheap and effective treatment by which ivory or bone that has become yellow can be restored to its original whiteness is to place the material requiring treatment for several days in a solution of one part of chloride of lime and four parts water. Ivory needs more time to whiten than does bone. At the expiration of the required period the ivory or bone is to be washed and allowed to dry off in a current of air."

Another method of whitening ivory given by Kunz from Dr. Artus is as follows:—Pour over the ivory a solution of five ounces of crystallized salt mixed with two pounds weight of soft water. Allow to stand for 36 to 48 hours and then wash the ivory several times in soft water. Then stand in a solution of ¾ of a pound of sodium sulphate to 2 pounds of water for 5 to 6 hours. Then an ounce of sodium acid diluted with 4 parts of water must be added gradually, the mixture stirred well and the vessel covered with a tight-fitting cover, and left for 36 hours. The liquid is finally poured off and the ivories washed in plain water. It is said that this can be repeated twice or more times, if the results are not completely satisfactory, and without harm to the pieces.

Softening of the ivory and making it transparent can be done by placing it in a solution of phosphoric acid of specific gravity of 1.130 and keeping in the solution until it becomes transparent. When washed and dried the ivory will become hard again but will soften on immersion in warm water. It is entirely unsatisfactory to use such a method in order to bend some delicate part of a carving and I do not believe the Chinese ever resorted to it. Possibly some action

110

of the soil helped to bring about the translucence of the Shang period hair-pins (See Pl. 4)

Of course the African ivory is denser and somewhat harder than Asiatic ivory and, therefore offers more resistance to the tools but it is less likely to chip, conditions being equal, and it takes a far better polish on the finished work. This polish is accomplished with the usual various abrasive papers, the finest sand paper, emery cloth, pumice and finally for a very high polish, rotten-stone or the finest rouge.

The staining of ivory has been practiced, as we have seen, since the earliest times, and although the natural color is certainly beautiful, no one can deny that the effect of economical use of soft colors is very much more interesting and the more so in that such staining does not lose the pattern of the grain but often makes it more prominent. I am unable at this time to get the actual facts concerning the colors used by the Chinese. One would be fairly safe in guessing, I should suppose, that they are related to those colors which they use in their paintings on paper, silk and wood. Dr. Kunz also gives certain notes which he has found concerning various European methods. The combinations of these follow:—

RED. The Chinese use cinnabar or mercury chloride (HgS) and the best is thought to come from Shansi province. This gives a yellow-red or vermillion which is inclined to darken somewhat on exposure to sunlight but when applied with a lacquer, is more permanent.

The Europeans use a formula of Brazil-wood chips boiled in alum-water. The filtered solution is applied to ivory which has previously been treated with a diluted solution of muriate of tin.

Another red stain is made of 4 parts of cochineal, 4 parts of cream of tartar, and 12 parts of tin solution. The cochineal is first dissolved in warm tin solution. Then the cream of tartar is added and finally a small amount of sal ammonia. This is applied direct.

Coral powder was used in China at least as early as Sung times and possibly even in T'ang times, but, though capable of producing a deep pink and even red, it is opaque and is not, I suppose, used on ivory.

Red lead (Minium) was also used in China. Its composition is $(PbO) 2PbO_2$ or Pb_3O_4 and it is yellower than cinnabar. It is also not permanent but has fair lasting qualities.

Red ochre (Umber) or limonite is a sort of iron oxide not containing water and is well known to both East and West. Its color is brownish-red but deep and permanent.

See also realgar described with orpiment (yellow).

BLUE. Azurite is the name given a number of compounds of copper. A typical formula is $2CuCO_3, Cu(OH)_2$ and its color is prussian blue or ultramarine, not a sky-blue. It has opacity but such brilliance that a thin solution might be used as a stain.

Ultramarine (lapis lazuli) is aluminum silicate, sodium, sulphur and sulphuric radical. The lapis lazuli of the East and of the West are alike, but its high cost made it customary to use a blue glass substitute in China. The real color is so strong that it could be used as a stain and it would be permanent.

Indigo is a vegetable pigment made from the indigo plant and is not quite so permanent as the above mineral colors. Yet it gives a very deep purple-blue which has been used for centuries in dyes and stains.

VIOLET. Violet can be obtained, according to Kunz, by first placing ivory for a few minutes in a much-diluted muriate of tin solution, and then letting it lay for an hour in a decoction composed of 50 parts Campeachy wood and 30 parts of water. This would, of course, not be a convenient stain with which to paint only small areas.

Violet stain can also be made, he says, by boiling for an hour 2 parts of Brazil-wood chips in 5 parts of water, filtering the decoction and mixing it with a solution of 12 parts of green vitriol to 25 parts of water.

He also gives a stain made of 1 part aniline violet dissolved in 10 parts of alcohol. We might add that any of the aniline colors could be so used but would be far from permanent and probably never were so used by the Chinese.

GREEN. Malachite is a clear, strong green and is very close to Azurite in composition, the formula being—$CuCo_3, Cu(OH)_2$—containing less copper carbonate than Azurite. It often occurs in nature in the same stone, certain areas being dark blue and others bright green. It has been used in China for centuries and though opaque is so brilliant that a stain can be made of it.

YELLOW. Orpiment is a sulphide of arsenic containing less arsenic than realgar, the composition being AsS while that of realgar is As_2S_3. The color of orpiment is brilliant yellow while that of realgar is "red as cockscomb." Both are soft looking and opaque but can be employed as stains. They cannot be mixed with lead white or they will darken. They are both poisonous, of course. Both have been used for centuries in China.

A yellow stain is given by Kunz as follows:— Soak 60 parts of finely ground curcuma root for a day in 500 parts of 80 percent alcohol and then filter through blotting paper.

He gives another of 95 parts of aniline yellow dissolved in 750 parts of 80 percent alcohol and again filtered. Both of these are fugitive.

Gamboge was not used very far back in China and was probably introduced from the West. It can be mixed with lead white, if so desired, and is fairly permanent under any conditions.

Yellow ochre gives a warm yellow color which has been used for centuries in China. Red ochre is made from it by burning. It is permanent.

BLACK. Lampblack (carbon black) is made

from the burning of various substances. There is even an "ivory black" made supposedly from the burning of ivory particles. Thus there are blacks from woods, bones etc. and all differ. Of course, the real lamp black was supposed to come from the burning of oil. It is all absolutely permanent and can be mixed with various oils, alcohol, lacquer etc.

Kunz gives the following:—Boil 1 part of finely cracked gallnuts, and 4 parts of pulverized verdigris, in 30 times their weight of water. Filter and reboil. After having been dipped in this solution the ivory has to be treated with another solution obtained by boiling 1 part Campeachy-wood extract (tied in a linen bag), 0.5 part gum arabic, 12 parts of water, and 12 parts of alum, for an hour, and then straining.

With this meagre information one could hardly be expected to set out to rival the Chinese in their beautiful craftsmanship in the carving and coloring of ivory. Our most skilled western carvers such as "Old Kaldenberg" as we used to call Mr. F. R. Kaldenberg and his master George Steffens could never rival the Chinese. Kaldenberg made a famous replica of the Venus de Milo and an ivory bust of Rembrandt, but when I knew him he was running a small shop in a loft, doing repairs and small, ornamental jobs for decorators. Even he was a second generation artist, as it were, for his father carved in ivory, amber, meerschaum and hard woods. Since he died and his establishment closed I think we have nobody in the whole western world who is a master of this art.

To give the reader a slight impression as to how simple the equipment the Chinese use actually is I am reproducing herewith 4 plates published by Arthur de Carle Sowerby in his article on "China's Ivory Carving Industry," reprinted from the China Journal of 1936. It is he to whom I am indebted not only for the general information I have quoted over his name frequently in this book but also for having done all of the special groundwork on the wonderful collection which I am privileged to show and which was made by Mr. and Mrs. Frank Lewis Hough.

112

INDEX